Work and Learning

An Introduction

Work and Learning

An Introduction

Bruce Spencer

Director of the Human Resources and Labour Relations (HRLR) Program at Athabasca University

Jennifer Kelly

Chair of the Department of Educational Policy Studies at the University of Alberta

Thompson Educational Publishing, Inc.

Toronto, Ontario

Information on how to obtain copies of this book is available at:

Website: www.thompsonbooks.com
E-mail: publisher@thompsonbooks.com
Telephone: (416) 766-2763
Fax: (416) 766-0398

Library and Archives Canada Cataloguing in Publication

Spencer, Bruce Work and learning : an introduction / Bruce Spencer and Jennifer Kelly.

Includes bibliographical references and index. ISBN 978-1-55077-232-6

1. Adult education--Textbooks. 2. Continuing education-- Textbooks. 3. Career development--Textbooks. I. Kelly, Jennifer II. Title.

LC5215.S65 2013 374'.01 C2013-901847-6

Production Editor: Katy Bartlett
Cover Design: Gary Blakeley, Blakeley Words+Pictures
Proofreader: Gillian Buckley

We acknowledge the support of the Government of Canada through the Canada Book Fund for our publishing activities.

Printed in Canada.

1 2 3 4 5 18 17 16 15 14 13

Table of Contents

About the Authors

Bruce Spencer is a Professor at Athabasca University's Centre for Interdisciplinary Studies. He is Director of the Human Resources and Labour Relations (HRLR) program and teaches courses in adult education and HRLR. Recent publications include: *The Purposes of Adult Education* and *Unions and Learning in a Global Economy,* both published by Thompson Educational Publishing.

Jennifer Kelly is a Professor and Chair of the Department of Educational Policy Studies at the University of Alberta. Her research areas are race, racialization, and the histories of racialized communities. Her present work includes mapping the Alberta history of African Canadian and other racialized workers. Her other publications include: *Under the Gaze: Learning to be Black in White Society* and *Borrowed Identities.*

Acknowledgments

This book is the culmination of twenty years or more of thinking, teaching, writing, reading, and attending conferences about work and learning–including the context within which it occurs, and the political, economic, and educational framework. It also draws on our experience and understandings of human resource management and labour relations, and educational policy and leadership, in and outside of the academy.

We wish to thank past and present staff and students at Athabasca University, the University of Alberta, and attendees at Researching Work and Learning international conferences and the conferences of the Canadian Association for the Study of Adult Education plus many other community and academic colleagues. Earlier versions of some of these chapters appeared in conference papers, appropriate journals and edited collections, as well as undergraduate and graduate course materials.

Introduction

This text will introduce you to some of the key understandings around work and learning. It will examine the claims made for this new area of study; it will discuss some of what we already know and point to what we don't know. Some work and learning scholars have overlooked the importance of "context" and "perspective" in influencing what and how adults learn at work–hence, in this introductory text there will be an emphasis on framing work and learning with these factors in mind.

The book is designed to challenge dominant perspectives but what you draw from this material will be up to you, it will depend on what you already know, on your reading, and on your values and attitudes. The work will be most useful if you are able to set aside some of the dominant ideas prevalent in society and explore new concepts and arguments.

The text has a Canadian focus but draws on global material and evidence–particularly from English-speaking countries and journals and texts written in English. The last chapter specifically examines work and learning aspects of the global workplace.

However, it should be recognized that the literature to draw on is extensive as "work and learning" ("learning at work," "workplace learning," "workplace education," "organizational learning," or other variants used to identify this field of study) is expansive going well beyond adult and continuing education, as Tara Fenwick explains:

> Workplace learning is fast becoming a central topic in fields that have little else in common. You can find its literature in journals of economics, innovation, organizational science, management/business studies, health care, and human-resource development (2006a, p. 187).

As a consequence this book should be of value to students and scholars from across all of these fields and associated areas of study that include a consideration of "work and learning" within their purview. Also as a consequence, this text draws on varied sources but cannot claim familiarity with all that has been written across disciplines. We are more familiar with work and learning studies presented at the biannual international conference *Researching Work and Learning* and the annual *Canadian Association for the Study of Adult Education* conference plus some general educational studies, labour relations, human resource management (HRM), human resource development (HRD), sociology, cultural studies and history conferences, journals and literature. Finally it should be noted that a number of terms and key concepts are explained in an effort to make the text accessible to all scholars regardless of disciplinary background.

Overview

The impetus to write a book of this kind has been building for some time. There are a number of recent edited collections that have served as introductory texts to the study of work and learning but, no matter how useful or insightful some of the contributions have been, these edited texts are not generally intended to provide a framework or lens with which to view the field. The only other introductory text was published in 2004 (Bratton, Helms-Mills, Pyrch & Sawchuk) and, although it has been very useful to date, it is more limited in scope than this introductory book. With growing interest in this field of study and large numbers of students registering for undergraduate Work and Learning courses, we felt it was time for another attempt at an introduction to this diverse field.

Inevitably this introduction reflects our concerns with this area of inquiry. Too often the importance and significance of the Human Resource Management (HRM) genesis of "work and learning" has been overlooked and this naturally provided a starting point for our text; in turn, this flowed into a consideration of managerial workplace culture and an analysis of the learning organization concept. We next turned to three areas that have generally not been carefully considered and in our view deserved attention—labour education and employee development schemes; the connection between work, political economy, and mass schooling; and an evaluation of the uses of "workplace learning" within both the workplace and the academy. Finally, we turned to look at aspects of training and skills, and at women and racialized minorities at work, before shifting our gaze to the global workplace and an example of what empowerment at work might look like, thus, providing a positive conclusion for readers.

It would be impossible to write one single introductory text that satisfied all the different disciplinary roots to such a diverse field of study as work and learning, or to find much common agreement amongst scholars as to what exactly makes up the core of this topic. This text is intended to meet a number of limited objectives: to provide an analytical approach to the field; to review the research and the literature; to explore the various lines of argument that have been made; to evaluate the available evidence; and to reflect on the various areas of inquiry. It suggests the need to investigate the corporate and political claims made for "work and learning," particularly from the perspective of worker empowerment. Hopefully this introductory text will provide insights and understandings; a foundation from which students (no matter what program of studies they are pursuing) can move towards a greater more critical exploration of the field.

Outline

These first three chapters can be considered as an introductory or context section focussed on perspectives on economy, work, management, and learning that underscore, but may not be explicit, in much of the study of work and learning.

Chapter 1 (Understanding the Human Resource Management/Corporate Connection) seeks to demystify some of the economic, work, and work-related learning context that is needed to understand this field of study. Terminology including globalization, the Canadian economy, gross domestic product (GDP), labour productivity, human capital theory, the knowledge economy, and human capital theory are introduced and explained. This introductory chapter to the field of study also immerses the reader in some of the key issues that underpin work and learning literature that are not always in the forefront. It looks at human resource management perspectives and at the arguments and assumptions behind the differences between industrial and post-industrial societies.

Chapter 2 (Organizational Culture and Organizational Learning) continues to reflect on the often ignored framing of work and learning literature by examining organizational culture and how that is learned. It also looks at the question "whose interest does this learning serve—employers, employees, or both?" The chapter discusses a number of debates including one centred on the potential impact of the pedagogics of work and learning and another on income inequality that are key, yet often overlooked, in the literature. It explains the concept of neo-liberalism, and sets it in the context of the recent financial and economic crisis.

Chapter 3 (The Learning Organization) is divided into three segments: a brief examination of groups and teams; a longer discussion of learning organizations; and a brief conclusion to the topic by reference to the applicability of the learning organization concept to contingent and precarious work. The chapter also examines the difference between work groups/teams and self-managed teams, and discusses what is implied by Taylorism. The chapter concludes with a review of two earlier significant texts on society, workplace learning, and education.

Chapters 4 to 6 can be grouped together insofar as they all look at aspects of "learning and schooling."

Chapter 4 (Workers' and Unions' Learning) opens with a brief discussion of workers' and unions' learning at work, before moving on to a longer exposition of what constitutes labour education—another key area of work and learning that is often under-reported. This is followed by an examination of employee development schemes (EDS) and a brief review of theoretical approaches to empowerment, workplace relations, and learning. Ideas and concepts discussed in this chapter include understanding unions, types of EDS, empowerment, and an argument for liberal adult education.

In Chapter 5 (From School to Work...) we take a step back to look at the connection between school and work. Our understanding of schooling for work starts from the inception of public schools and then moves the discussion forward to review education from the 1930s to the 1990s. This is followed by a section on neo-conservative re-structuring from the 1990s to the present. In tracing these developments we also look at the concepts of progressive education (including the ideas of John Dewey) back to basics, including accountability and standardized testing that all form part of the neo-conservative schooling agenda. We explain the concept of the "hidden curriculum" and also attempt an explanation of the different political and sociological ideologies that underpinned the arguments that schooling should essentially be a preparation for work.

Chapter 6 (...And Workplace Learning to School) begins with a discussion of an example of the use of workplace prior learning assessment and recognition (PLAR) and then reviews what PLAR is. This review leads into a discussion of adult learning. Some of the problems with PLAR and credentialism are discussed next—these issues are usually ignored in discussions of PLAR. We also explain the difference between critical thinking and critical thought and whether or not PLAR increases access to higher education. The section on workplace learning and PLAR argues that PLAR is an important component of the work and learning debate both at work and in post-secondary institutions (further and higher education) and recognizes that mature student entry and the recognition of experiential learning will have an effect on those educational institutions that are open to these arguments. The chapter concludes the PLAR debate by making the case for a sensitive, more thoughtful discourse on the limits and possibilities of PLAR. The final section takes a brief look at work and learning in the academy itself.

The final two chapters look at some outstanding issues and possible resolutions; introducing a global dimension and a possible change agenda.

In Chapter 7 (Transitions, Gender, and Difference: Training and Skills) we will introduce a matrix of workplace learning issues ranging from the position of women and cultural difference at work to approaches to training and skills. We begin with the idea that work and learning can be viewed from the lens of "transitions," including considering the role and value of volunteering as job preparation, and as a way of viewing technology and training. In two further sections we discuss gender and difference at work, and skills and training, as well as explaining the idea of competency-based training.

Chapter 8 (The Challenge of Democratizing Work and Learning in a Global Economy) is centrally concerned with the challenges of democratizing work and learning, empowering workers, and responding to the problems of globalization. We open with an example of work in the globalized economy, what it means to shift production to the "economic south" and specifically the Spectrum Sweater factory collapse that cost sixty-two lives and multiple injuries. We attempt to draw some conclusions from that tragedy. The next section begins with a discussion on the democratization of work with a few observations before reviewing the ideas behind participatory strategic human resource management (HRM). This is followed by examining an example of empowerment at work—the Mondragon co-operatives of northern Spain. We outline the co-operatives' success in meeting their original purpose of creating jobs and examine Mondragon's record on running the co-operatives. The final section reviews the experience of the co-operatives during recession and growth before progressing to a brief discussion on other co-operatives and of how Mondragon is being considered as an example of worker-centred economic development and worker empowerment in North America and beyond.

CHAPTER 1

Understanding the Human Resource Management/Corporate Connection

This first chapter seeks to demystify some of the economic/work and learning context and terminology that is needed to understand this field of study. Terminology including globalization, the Canadian economy, gross domestic product (GDP), labour productivity, human capital theory, the knowledge economy, and human capital theory are introduced and explained. This introductory chapter also immerses you in some of the key issues that underpin work and learning literature. It looks at human resource management perspectives, arguments, and assumptions behind the differences between industrial and post-industrial societies. The chapter concludes with a discussion of the significance of the often used phrase "our employees are our most valuable resource."

Introduction

It can be argued that to a large extent the current interest in "work and learning," and more specifically the "learning organization," has its genesis in Peter Senge's work, particularly the 1990 text *The Fifth Discipline: The Art and Practice of the Learning Organization*. What is often overlooked when acknowledging this work is that this (and other similar texts) are entirely "managerialist" (or functional) in perspective—it's all about making the organization efficient and profitable from a managers' perspective with employees regarded as a "human resource" input, whose knowledge and learning are to be in the service of the organization. Presented in this way it is essentially an argument for human resource management rather than for employee development.

The link between corporate HRM and workplace learning is more often as not ignored, if not assumed, in the work and learning literature, be it in the study of adult education, management, economics, or any of the disciplines or subdisciplines where work and learning is discussed. We will critically examines this connection and looks again at HRM perspectives and supporting arguments.

To reveal the link between HRM and workplace learning and expose it to examination sometimes feels like "breaking the spell" cast over the wonderment of learning at work. To explore this further we shall discuss the topic with occasional reference to an HRM approach to work and learning as revealed in a typical HRM textbook. At the time of writing the most popular text in Canada at present is *Canadian Human Resource Management: A Strategic Approach* by Hermann Schwind, Hari Das, and Terry Wagar. Its popularity is probably due to the fact that all authors are Canadian (it is not a Canadian version of a US text) and it is very current in its content.

The various editions of this textbook are comprehensive and wide-ranging, and draw extensively on Canadian material. The introduction to the text discusses the strategic importance of HRM and human resource planning and it serves as a useful introduction to the field and to the way it is viewed today. However, these works are not particularly reflective about the context of HRM or critical of its purpose; the author's perspective represents the dominant corporate company view of economy and society. The authors discuss the importance of HRM and why HRM has come to play such a central role in private- and public-sector organizations.

The thrust of the book is that HRM and workplace learning is not only a necessary managerial function it is also vital for organizational success. A critical "workplace learners" perspective on HRM is not offered in the text.

HRM Perspectives

To be sure, HRM as a field of study has attracted some criticism. While it might generally be agreed that organizations should, for example, observe basic employment equity and health and safety legislation, some critics argue that the HRM function is too often used to ensure only minimum compliance. A more severe criticism could relate to the company's products (e.g., cigarettes) or use of natural resources (e.g., clear-cut forestry), and might argue that all HRM does is ensure workers' compliance in these "harmful" company activities.

The recent development of HRM as a central plank in company policy, designed to give companies the "cutting edge" vis à vis the competition by involving workers more in company activities, has heightened another criticism. This criticism is that HRM has always been concerned with maximizing the output from employees, and recent attempts to increase the involvement of workers in some aspects of company decision-making are designed ultimately to maximize company output and profit. Therefore, this application of HRM is essentially consensual in its method of operation: it assumes that there are common interests between employers and employees (a unitarist view), and denies that sometimes there might be divergent interests (a pluralist view), or that employees in one company might have common interests (some would say "class" interests) with workers in other companies (a conflict view). For some critics, HRM is only necessary because, in an historical sense, labour (human resources) has been separated from owning and controlling the productive process, and therefore needs to be "managed" (Ellerman, 1990).

The fact that many companies now recognize labour unions and involve HRM specialists in formulating and administering labour agreements does not undermine this critique–in fact, it underscores the point. In negotiations, the function of the HRM department is to support management negotiators, and after completion of the agreement, HRM will try to ensure worker and union compliance with the contract, and to prevent any further encroachment on management rights.

Some commentators argue that current HRM practices are much more humanistic than the alternatives, and that work in many modern companies is fulfilling–certainly more so than in earlier times. The authors of the Schwind, Das, and Wagar textbook share this perspective, but this viewpoint is not a universal one. There are alternative viewpoints; for example, some critics hold that most work in modern society is dehumanizing, that the competitiveness of modern organizations leads to the development of less fulfilling social relationships, and that the strategic HRM function supports this dominant and destructive activity.

The Schwind, Das, and Wagar text goes on to explain the "two greatest challenges" facing Canada are the "global trade challenge" and the importance of "productivity increases." Mastering these is seen as essential if "Canada" is to have a prosperous future. It also discusses changes towards a "knowledge" economy and assumes a shift towards a post-industrial society. Other texts may approach an introduction differently but these approaches have now become common elements within mainstream HRM/HRD textbooks. On the other hand, the trends and changes are assumed but rarely examined.[1]

Globalization, Canada, and Productivity

The term globalization is used extensively today in many different contexts. Globalization in this context refers to the internationalizing of trade, production, and capital. Some companies will choose to relocate their production facilities wherever they can find cheaper labour and lower taxes, others may choose to no longer directly produce anything but buy and market the goods produced to their specifications. Nike might be a good example of this approach. Finance capital is even more mobile; financial institutions can move their resources to wherever they can get the highest returns.[2]

No one will deny the importance of economic globalization, particularly in respect to the freedom for corporations to move around financial capital and locate production facilities worldwide. But the impact of globalization is often overstated as a way of suggesting that global economic forces cannot be contested by national governments or citizens either acting alone or in concert with other nations and peoples. It should also be remembered that Canada has always been a "trading nation" and was developed economically to serve the needs of Britain for furs, wheat, and lumber and today trades most of its exports to the USA with resource and extraction industries still being dominant in that trade. Both of these points are essentially missing from the introduction to the textbook.

Another aspect not discussed is the impact of economic activity on the health and safety of workers and on the environment. Canada may lead the world in asbestos production, but it also has

---

1 A couple of UK texts are more critical in orientation, for examples: Bratton & Gold, *Human Resource Management: Theory and Practice*, 5th ed., 2012; and Storey, *Human Resource Management: A Critical Text*, 3rd ed., 2007. There is also a *Routledge Companion to Human Resource Management*, edited by Storey, Wright, and Ulrich, 2009, to accompany the Storey text. All these draw from "critical management studies" but at the time of writing there are no known equivalent Canadian texts.

2 The idea that we have to accept the globalization of trade, production, and finance as a "fact of life," not to be challenged by individuals, workers' organizations or countries, is part of the dominant ideology of neo-liberal economics. However, the global financial crisis of 2008 and subsequent economic crisis in the US and Europe may cause some questioning of the wisdom of unfettered economic globalization.

more workers dying a painful death due to exposure to asbestos dust. Nickel and zinc production comes at a cost to the environment, as does the production of newsprint (all these industries are highlighted on page 5 of the Schwind, Das, and Wagar textbook with the negatives ignored). Many would argue that government should toughen up safety and health, and environmental legislation on the grounds that organizations, if left unregulated, will not incur the costs needed to meet the needs of Canadians. The importance of national government and supra-government organizations, such as the European Union, developing environmental regulations is now more widely argued—see for example J. Freedland, 2006. It is argued that they did not do so in the past and, if these organizations are self-regulating, will not do so in the future.

The "Canadian economy" is a collective term used to describe all economic activity taking place in Canada. It includes all firms and services, whether or not they are Canadian owned and controlled (for example, Walmart and McDonald's stores in Canada are included even though they are US owned and controlled). The economy encompasses publicly provided services, co-operatives, not-for-profit organizations, privately owned family firms and companies and publicly owned (shareholder-owned) corporations. However, it is misleading to suggest that increases in overall Canadian productivity is automatically a key to economic welfare. Some of these companies may be moving resources across borders without fully accounting for them, while others may outsource, no matter what productivity increases are achieved, simply to access cheap labour elsewhere. This outsourcing can include services as well as production and knowledge jobs as well as brawn or sweated labour. Even if there are overall increases in economic wellbeing, there is no guarantee such benefits will be equitably distributed.

For example, a key aspect, which is seldom discussed, is the use of off-shore tax-free banking by corporations and wealthy individuals. Successive Canadian governments have refused to rein in the use of off-shore tax havens, and, in some cases, have even been responsible for the development of these facilities, thereby allowing money to flow in and out of these accounts tax free (Deneault, 2011). The *Tax Justice Network* calculates there is something between 21–32 trillion dollars (or 10–15% of all global money) owned by 0.1% of the global population stashed away in tax havens. This tax avoidance costs 280 billion dollars in public revenue (two to three times the size of all global aid budgets) or 20% in lost Canadian tax revenue (Henry, 2012).

Industrial and Post-Industrial Societies

As you read more mainstream HRM and work and learning literature you will come across many references suggesting that we now live in a "post-industrial," "post-modern," or even "post-capitalist" society compared to a few years ago (for most authors the changeover occurs in the late 1970s). Accounts vary but the suggestion of a fundamental shift in the way the economy is structured also refers to an "information age" or a new "knowledge-based" economy as being dominant, and to the nature of work as having been transformed from "Fordist" or "Taylorist" (typified as factory assembly line jobs, very specific, routine with few learning opportunities) to participatory, flexible, multi-tasked knowledge-rich jobs.

For example, it is worth reflecting on the changes that have taken place in the Canadian economy. Yes, Canada has moved from being dominantly a primary producer of agricultural produce and raw materials to an industrial nation and now to a predominantly service sector economy but not as definitively as it might seem. If we look at the changes in terms of the contribution of the primary sector (agriculture, mining, fishing, etc.), the secondary sector (manufacturing and construction), and the tertiary sector (services, personal and financial, entertainment, etc.) to Gross Domestic Product (GDP) the major decline is within the primary sector of the economy. Agriculture, fishing, and traditional mining have all declined as a proportion of GDP. The secondary sector is still important and the value produced within it continues to rise in real terms even as it too declines proportionately in GDP terms. We do not eat, live in, drive, or wear "knowledge"; the so-called knowledge economy may affect the way all of these things are produced but they still are produced either in Canada or elsewhere. Also noteworthy is the stability of extraction activity—oil and gas, wood (and pulp production), mining (after allowing for the decline in coal and iron ore)—in real value terms within GDP, and the importance of these in Canadian trade (for example, half of all Canadian oil and more than three-quarters of natural gas production is exported). Canada trades about 30% of its GDP (the Schwind, Das, and Wagar textbook refers to 44% of GDP "coming from exports," on page 6, a figure they got from *Time* magazine, but that figure is not borne out by other sources or indeed by the authors' pie chart on page 15 constructed from Statistics Canada figures) and more than two-thirds of that trade is with the USA (almost three quarters of all exports go to the USA and approximately 50% of all imports come from the USA (CIA World Fact-book, 2012). Canada is part of the "global economy," as it has been from the export of furs and wheat to oil and gas and the import of other foodstuffs and manufacturing goods, but the overwhelming majority of the goods and services produced in Canada are consumed in Canada, which is similar to the situation in other developed economies (GDP trends and details are outlined at the end of this chapter).

Another key question is whether the nature of work and "organizations" has changed that much for the majority of workers and for others who experience them. Do fast-food or e-commerce employees (whether or not they are described as "associates" or "partners") have very different and more satisfying jobs than factory workers? Is there more or less job security in the economy? Can that be described as "flexibility" or should it be described as a lack of corporate commitment to the workforce? Are the key decisions in the organization (be it public or private) taken at the top or are they "shared" with the workforce in some way? A six-country study argued: "In most cases, employee representatives are merely informed of upcoming changes by management with no input into decision making" (Freeman et al., 2007, p. 177). Who owns and controls the organization? Who gets rich from its activity and is anyone, society or the environment, harmed in any way as a result of its activity?

The textbooks on HRM are often "light" on the discussion of these issues, as if there are no real issues of power and control. However, readers should not suspend their critical understandings and their everyday experience of the real world when reviewing this literature.[3]

A 2003 report by Statistics Canada (Beckstead & Gellatly) charting the changes in the Canadian economy acknowledges that less than 20% of the total workforce are employed in "knowledge" occupations—and many of these are "old" rather than "new" knowledge occupations such as physicians, dentists, engineers, or lawyers

[3] In fairness to Schwind, Das, and Wagar, they do occasionally mention the limitations of some corporate employee involvement strategies from a workers' perspective (for example, from employers "stressing the system" (p. 471)), but they quickly move on.

(p. 35-36). Information and communications technologies (ICT) and science areas represents approximately 10% of the Canadian economy and, while perhaps 50% of jobs in those areas may be described as knowledge jobs, only 1 in 8 new service jobs outside of ICT and science areas can be described as knowledge jobs (p. 37). They also point out that knowledge jobs in the other 90% of the economy have actually declined to about 12% at the time of their survey compared to 17% in 1981.

It's important to acknowledge that all workers have knowledge and apply it at work. However, Statistics Canada is noting what workers have been reporting on for some time: opportunities to apply knowledge at work is in decline, "deskilling" rather than "reskilling" is the norm and workers' knowledge is underemployed. While there may be specific skill shortages, generally Canada has a knowledgeable workforce but not the jobs to match it (Livingstone, 1999a). This is a situation mirrored in other Western countries and multiplied ten times over in many developing economies. The assumption that most future employment will involve knowledge work is questionable.

Productivity Revisited

In economics, "productivity" or more accurately "labour productivity" is a simple measure of the production output in relation to amount of labour input. When commentators talk about Canada's productivity falling or rising they are usually taking a crude measure of the value of output—GDP—and comparing that to the size of the labour force or the total number of hours worked by Canadians in paid employment.[4]

The importance of labour productivity in growth, competitiveness, and trade is closely allied to the workplace learning agenda

[4] A feature article in the *Globe and Mail* (Jan. 30, 2010) by Kevin Lynch, former clerk of the Privy Council and secretary to the Cabinet, titled "Canada's Productivity Trap" displays all the usual concern about the decline in Canada's productivity performance but fails to examine the relative decline in Canadian manufacturing jobs, questions of ownership and control of real investment in companies in Canada and those company resources, or the outsourcing of the most "productive" jobs. By ignoring all these and other key structural questions, the article predictably concludes by calling for more competition, less government, more flexibility, closer links between universities and industry, more "knowledge work," and more globalization. In other words, an acceleration of all the forces in play over the last twenty years that have led to the current situation!

in the HRM literature but it is very rarely examined. Productivity in different sectors of the economy can vary enormously and, as a generalisation, the more capital a worker has to work with the more productive she or he will appear to be. As a result, manufacturing activity appears to be more productive than most services. Manufacturing jobs are the most "productive" in Canada, that is because the machinery and technology (i.e., what economists refer to as capital) that support each job results in high value output, particularly compared to service jobs. If companies maintain technology investments, workers productivity can rise; if they run down a plant, move processes to the US or overseas, and/or close plants, Canada's labour productivity falls. In general, countries that are most successful at defending a large manufacturing base have higher average productivity growth. This therefore requires an active industry policy (building up a manufacturing base) which is of course critical if training and retraining is to be successful.[5]

There is also the question of the value of the product as measured by the market. An interesting example is provided in Alberta's oil-sands. The huge pieces of capital employed at the oil-sands results in high labour output in the production process, for example, one giant truck driven by one driver replaces six or more standard sized trucks and drivers (none of which is related to "learning" as such). If oil prices are high, the driver will appear to be more productive (recording "increased productivity") than when oil prices are lower (recording "lower productivity") not due to anything the driver is doing. The driver may be shifting the exact same quantity of tar sands, but because the value of his/her output as measured by the market has changed so has his/her "productivity." In addition, some of the older technology may use as much as two units of energy to produce three but that net gain of one unit of energy can be valued highly in the volatile oil and gas market.

Sticking with this example it should be noted that most of the environmental and social costs associated with the oil-sands production are not borne by the companies, such as the now infamous "tailings ponds." These huge company-made polluted water areas, more "lakes" than "ponds," are "externalities" in economic terms.

---

[5] The GDP figures at the end of this chapter show that 22% of GDP comes from 13% of the workforce in manufacturing and 71% of GDP comes from 76% of the workforce in tertiary employment—a rough guide indicating that manufacturing jobs boost productivity calculations.

They are not accounted for in company finances or in productivity calculations. Joel Bakan (2004, p. 70) quotes leading US businessman Robert Monks (a twice-run Republican Senate candidate) "the corporation is an externalizing machine in the same way as a shark is a killing machine" he argues its not "malevolence" but simply what corporations do and is "potentially very, very damaging to society." Ray Anderson, another successful businessman, had a similar revelation about how the modern day corporation was an "instrument of destruction" "externaliz(ing) any cost that an unwary or uncaring public will allow it to externalize" (Bakan, p. 71). In his case he set about making wholesale changes in the way his company produced carpets: unfortunately his example remains an exception.

Productivity linked workplace learning theory is important because of the central role it gives to HRM/workplace learning via human capital theory (for a critique of human capital theory, see Bouchard, 1998; 2006). The argument is that if workers can increase their own human capital via training, workplace learning, and, as argued more recently, investments in emotional labour, then productivity can rise. For example the 2007 Conference Board of Canada publication, *Learning and development outlook: Are we learning enough?* (Hughes & Grant) argues:

> Canada's productivity is lagging behind that of its competitors. One strategy Canadian organizations are using to meet these challenges is the renewal and upgrading of their workers' skills. By spending on TLD to build workers' skills, organizations seek to create enough additional human capital to make themselves more competitive (p. 1).

But they also report on low spending rates on training, learning, and development (TLD) by Canadian organizations (most companies training needs are modest), which is a reflection of the nature of most work and capital investment in Canada—few skilled workers need apply!

A Note on Human Capital Theory

The contribution of education and training to overall economic development and growth, as well as to an individual's economic future, has been recognized for some time. However, the idea that education is an important contributor to economic growth, and therefore a primary purpose of education should be to support the economy, was highlighted in the late 1950s and early 1960s. It was during this period of "full employment" in the main Western economies that attention turned to increasing the productivity of existing labour through training and retraining and through more targeted education of existing and future labour. It was argued that education could be divided into "investment" and "consumption" activities and that state funds should primarily support investment in "human capital."

The skills and knowledge that working people gained through education and training, through formal, non-formal, and informal learning activities was likened to a form of "capital" resulting from deliberate investments. These investments in human capital were held to be the major reason for the faster more developed state of modern economies (Schultz, 1961). What followed from this argument was a view that countries should control the expansion and the mix of their education system in order to maximize economic growth. This human capital theory had clear implications for schools and the formal higher education system and also for adult education in general. It pushed all of them to justify their educational activity in economic terms, as opposed to liberal educational ones.

Not only were the relative costs of different education programs examined but arguments were made as to the "rate-of-return" that a particular education course (an investment) could expect to yield and what investments (education) should be made to fulfil "manpower forecasts." The arguments that economic development hinged on these investments, and that education should be in the service of economy, essentially in the service of capitalist production, was hotly debated (Shaffer, 1961). However, human capital theory has remained as an important starting point for many in the work and learning literature (Hart, 1995, p. 20; Bouchard, 1998; 2006)

A second conclusion from human capital theory is the individualising of the above argument: if workers wanted good jobs and to avoid unemployment they had to "invest" in their own education and learning (this was no longer primarily a state responsibility). Generally, and obviously there is a correlation between more education and better jobs but there are no guarantees, it also avoids discussion about what quality work is available even if workers increase their "human capital."

A third focus is on human capital at the level of the organization. If employees can learn at work and contribute to organizational learning, then the human capital of the organization will grow and the company prosper. These assumptions about the "learning organization" and what benefits that may bring to workers needs to be critically examined. (This will be explored in the next two chapters.)

"Our Employees Are our Most Valuable Resource"

This phrase of course has become the mantra of modern corporations. (Schwind, Das, and Wagar claim that 4 of the top 5 strategic priorities of corporations identified by leading CEOs are HR-related, p. 8.) What is not clear is how many companies actually believe or act as if they really mean it. It places the functions of HR departments' right at the centre of corporate activity and therefore writers on HR and work and learning can perhaps be excused for not wanting to subject the statement to close scrutiny. If the above statement is true, then HRM and workplace learning really is important. However, when a company gets into trouble, it usually "downsizes," often the first action is to lay-off or sack workers. The work may then be "outsourced," never to return. These actions may be partially determined by market circumstances, but whatever it is that is driving company policy, whenever this happens, it should call into question their assertion that "employees are our most valuable resource."

Some organizations may well believe that the company's "competitive advantage" depends on a happy committed workforce and thus may work towards that end (full-time employees, higher skills, job flexibility, workplace learning, focus on knowledge work–sometimes referred to as the "high road"). Others may equally believe that tight control of labour costs combined with close supervision over employees is the road to success (low-paid, part-time employees, routine jobs–a "low road"). Both approaches can work "equally well" (Bratton et al., 2004, p. 71). Being an HR professional in the first organization may well be more satisfying than in the second. Survey research suggests that "empowering" workers does not generally affect the bottom line as imagined by many authors, although more say and participation at work can influence employee loyalty (Freeman et al., 2007).

An organization may work hard to involve its employees, perhaps referring to them as "associates" or "partners" and developing "open door" policies, as trumpeted by Walmart. But it does not follow that they will be well rewarded. An article in *The Wall Street Journal* (Zimmerman, March 26, 2004) under the heading "Costco's

Dilemma: Be Kind To Its Workers, or Wall Street?" contrasts Costco's more generous salary and benefits package to that of Walmart's "parsimonious approach to employee compensation." According to the article, some analysts and investors claim Costco's generosity to its employees is at the expense of shareholders and that shareholders' interests come first (in law, shareholders have no responsibility to other stakeholders). Walmart is renowned for its policy of driving down supplier costs regardless of the impact that has on the workers in less developed economies that are making the products for its stores in North America. Its aggressive marketing (big box stores), low wage policies, and anti-unionism have met opposition in North America, but its shareholders are happy: earnings per share are significantly higher than at Costco.

Again, HRM professionals work in both companies.

Canadian GDP Details and Trends

The major change in Gross Domestic Product, as noted earlier, has been in relation to the relative importance of the primary sector of the economy. Agriculture, fishing, and traditional mining have all declined as a proportion of GDP. Primary production is down from 26% in 1920 to about 10% by 1960, 7% by 1990, and 5% by 2011 (but the real dollar value of the sector continues to increase thanks mainly to extraction activities). The secondary sector rose to about 30% by 1920 and stayed at about or just below that level till 1970 with a slight decline to 25% by 1990, and 22% by 2011 (again, the real dollar value of manufacturing output has increased up to 2008).

The biggest change is in the relative importance of the tertiary sector, from about 35% in 1920 to 58% in 1990 and 71% by 2011. (There is an"other" category used in these GDP statistics which hovers between 3% and 10% depending on the reporting methods—calculations for 2011 largely ignore the "other" category.)

The important point to note here is that industrial production was never really dominant. Even in the key period of "industrialisation," the tertiary sector was a larger contributor to GDP than industry. And although Canada was never as industrial as some other economies, it is not so very different in this regard. Industrial activity (especially if you subtract construction) was typically no more than a third of any Western countries' economic activity. (The data for this and the following paragraphs is taken from Finkel and Conrad, 1993, particularly chapters 8 and 11; Wotherspoon, 2009, Chapter 6; CIA World Factbook, 2012; and Statistics Canada, 2012.)

It can be argued that much of the previous primary and more importantly tertiary sector activity was geared towards the needs of industrialisation and that today the tertiary sector is generating its own needs separate from industrial requirements. The growth in information technology is an example in point. Also manufacturing employment levels have continued to decline (about 25% of the workforce worked in industry until the mid 1960s, down to 15% by the mid 1990s, and 13% by 2008). Likewise, employment in services (not including public administration) has tripled since the Second World War (37% of the workforce by the mid 1990s); the total for all tertiary employment was 76% by 2008. (The CIA World Fact-book 2012 notes these proportions but it is not clear as to which year the data was collected.) The result is a significant change over this time period in the nature of work. But the point remains: the shift is not so much from industrial to post-industrial as from primary production to tertiary.

We have also seen that the recession resulting from the 2008 financial crisis has led to a major and continuing loss of full-time and well-paid Canadian manufacturing jobs and, as argued above, a decline in Canada's comparative "national productivity" calculations.

CHAPTER 2

Organizational Culture and Organizational Learning

This chapter examines "organizational culture" and how that is promoted and learned. It also looks at the question of whose interest does this organizational culture learning serve—employers, employees, or both. The chapter discusses a number of debates that are key, yet often overlooked, in the literature: one centred on the impact of the pedagogics of work and learning and another on income inequality. It explains the concept of neo-liberalism, and sets it in the context of the recent financial and economic crisis. The chapter concludes by reflecting on the perspectives taken in the first two chapters and relating those to Canadian work and learning literature and to questions of power and control. The final section explains informal and non-formal learning, which may be useful to those who do not have an adult education background.

Learning Organizational Culture

Workers have always learned at work; learning at work is not a new phenomena. What they have learned has always been diverse. For example, it ranges from learning about the job and how to do the work, to how to relate to fellow workers, supervisors, and bosses (the social relations of work), to gaining understandings about the nature of work itself and how work has a bearing on the kind of society we live in.

Workers, generally speaking, have always tried to make meaning out of their work experience (see for examples Terkel, 1977; Sennet, 1998). It's difficult for someone to spend eight hours a day, five days a week, doing something in a totally detached way, and even more difficult if a person hates every minute of it. Read most accounts of workers describing their work and this becomes clear. Workers have always wanted to do a good job, even if that job is menial; the new emphasis on workplace learning should always take this into account. In addition, workers would like to have influence on how work is organized and on the running of organizations. A survey of six primarily English-speaking countries reported on workers in all countries as wanting to have a greater say in company decision making and participatory processes (Freeman et al., 2007).

However, workers are naturally encouraged to learn about what is useful for the employer, and some of their learning may contribute to a "culture of silence" (Freire, 1970), that is, to an acceptance of the way things are (or becoming "neo-liberal selves," as described by Davies and Petersen, 2005, when discussing this phenomena in the academy). For example, they may come to accept the corporate idea that we are all part of a global economy and that the organization must strive to out-compete others in the workplace and outside it, in order to survive.[1]

To ignore power and authority at work is to ignore the realities of what it is to be an employee. Power shapes structures of control and organizational culture. Managerially determined organizational culture is imposed; Edgar Schein, Professor at the MIT Sloan School of Management defines organizational culture as:

> the pattern of basic assumptions that a given group has invented, discovered, or developed in learning to cope with its problems of external adaptation and internal integration, and that have worked well enough to be considered valid, and, therefore, to be taught to new members as the correct way to perceive, think, and feel in relation to those problems (1985, 12).

Not all definitions of organizational culture will be as clearly stated in relation to managerial power as that of Schein's. He notes that assumptions have to be "valid" and a "correct way to perceive, think, and feel," therefore it is clear in practice that organizational culture is something to be determined and molded by management. For most workers, organizational culture is what management says it is. Employees are expected "to be on the same page," to accept the mission statement of the organization, and to "buy into" the organizational goals. Learning about that culture is learning to accept it. (In some situations of course workers are capable of developing

[1] A good example of this kind of workplace learning is provided in the Michael Moore film *Sicko* when he interviews former US insurance/health maintenance organization executives who explain how they "learned" to deal with clients making insurance claims. They basically learned how to undermine these claims and make them ineligible, even when they were legitimate. As one interviewee explained, the more they learned and the more successful they became in declining customers' sick and injury claims, the more they were rewarded with higher salaries.

local work-group counter-cultures—a processes that can be facilitated by union organization and collective ideas.)

John Storey, a leading business school professor in the UK, has commented that the "management of culture" has become a distinguishing feature of HRM, and dates the "remarkable trend" away from "personnel procedures and rules" to the "management of culture" to the early to mid-1990s (Storey, 2001, p. 8). He comments that "managing cultural change and moving towards HRM can often appear to coincide and become one and the same project." Corporate cultural management is "perceived to offer the key to unlocking of consensus, flexibility and commitment."

This perspective is evident in Senge's early claim that these new HRM policies create a "sense of shared ownership" and control of the enterprise (1990, p. 13) and Wellins, Byham, and Wilson's argument that employees feel a "sense of job ownership" (1991, pp. 10–11). It is restated recently by Eric Newell's comment "really, what we are trying to do is engage people to get them thinking like owners of the business" (quoted in Schwind et al., 2007, p. 471).[2] Peter Senge also emphasizes that the role of the "leader" (i.e., manager) is "to help people restructure their views of reality" (1990, p. 3). All this may appear innocent, but the "sense of ownership," however, is of course not the same thing as workers actually owning and controlling and could be regarded as a form of propaganda.

The idea behind this shift in managerial strategies is that consensus would displace conflict (and collective bargaining), flexibility (a "substitute term for greater management control," [Storey, 2001, p. 8]) would increase productivity, and commitment would lift labour performance higher—"committed employees would 'go the extra mile' in pursuit of customer service and organizational goals," (Storey, 2001, p. 8). To achieve all of this means changing a whole set of workers' behaviours, attitudes, and values, displacing a "pluralist" (with different interests that sometimes coincide and sometimes conflict) and quasi democratic culture (with unions challenging management decisions in collective bargaining) with a "unitarist" (with everyone in the organization assumed to be sharing exactly the same goals) and a "democratic" culture (with claims of "empowerment" and "teams").

---

2 Former Chairman and CEO of Syncrude Canada Ltd. and past-Chancellor of the University of Alberta.

Critical scholars have argued that a robust corporate culture provides behaviour "scripts" for workers to follow. These "scripts," written by management, reflect the big issues of productivity, flexibility, and commitment, and can be used to capture and manage workers' "emotional labour" (Du Gay, 1996a).

The Pedagogics of Work and Learning

In September 1999 the First International Conference on Researching Work and Learning was held at Leeds University, England. It was hosted by the School of Continuing Education, the location of more than twenty years of research with and by working people into the conditions of work, unemployment, and the relationship between work and community. Much of the Leeds work had been conducted directly with labour unions and union members at the workplace. Nevertheless, Keith Forrester, the leading Leeds researcher admits that:

> we too have not attached sufficient weight to the inter-relationship between employee learning, new management practices and the wider "modernising" strategies currently being pursued by New Labour in this country, and to a lesser extent, in a number of other countries (Forrester, 1999, p. 188).

If they missed it at Leeds—with its focus on workers' interests—it is perhaps not surprising that it has been overlooked more generally in the workplace learning literature, much of which claims either a neutral position or assumes more overtly a managerial perspective. The enthusiasm for "lifelong learning," the "learning society," and "learning organizations" has blurred researchers' critical gaze as to what exactly is going on in workplace learning.

Forrester defines the problem in the following terms:

> In the increased competitive pressure on management to improve the quality and quantity of the labour input, the notion of employee subjectivity (affective elements such as initiative, "emotional labour" [customer care], values and attitudes, intra-individual management, self actualisation and adaptability) has emerged as a key area of new management and thinking and that workplace or work-related learning is often seen as an essential part of "capturing" employee subjectivity in achieving corporate objectives. The wider socio-economic changes of recent decades has resulted in many workplaces questioning aspects of the tradi-

> tionalist "Taylorist" division between thinking and doing along with the rigidities characteristic of a Fordist workplace regime. *However, instead of the brave new world of employee "empowerment," "autonomy," satisfaction and fulfilment within those "new workplaces" or "workplaces of the future" there is just as likely, we suggest, to emerge new mechanisms of oppression and managerial control. If this is the case, or at least a possibility, then there is the danger that the equally brave new world of pedagogics in relation to "work and learning" will become part of the new forms of oppression and control in the workplace* (Forrester, 1999, p. 188. *Emphasis added*).

Of particular importance here is Forrester's observation that the increased competitive pressure on management to improve the quality and quantity of the labour input can result in "new forms of oppression and control in the workplace" rather than empowerment or increased worker control. Forrester's observation is supported by a study of workplace skills training policies in Australia and Aotearoa/New Zealand:

> The resulting reforms have had a remarkably unilateral effect: they move control over and benefits from skill training away from individuals and unions and into the hands of private capital (Jackson & Jordan, 2000, p. 195).

Bratton (1992) has suggested that the learning organization claim of empowerment for workers is contradicted by close electronic surveillance of operating activities resulting in "computer-controlled autonomy." And that employers are caught between two contradictory imperatives: regulating workers' activity too tightly undermines workers learning and creative potential, whereas empowering workers undermines employer and management control. Evidence from the UK would also suggest that strong union organization is needed to take advantage of more expansive workplace learning opportunities and even the new legislated Union Learning Representatives (discussed in Chapter 4) are in danger of becoming "corporate" or "state" rather than "worker" conduits for learning (Shelley & Calveley, 2007; Forrester & Li, 2009).

Learning for Whose Interests?

Few of those who write about workplace learning adequately deal with the criticism that issues of power and control have largely been ignored in mainstream writing. For example, David Boud and John Garrick, in their introduction to the popular collection of readings *Understanding Learning at Work*, discuss some of the negative impact of workplace learning's "market driven emphasis" but also argue for the close connection between "productivity and the operation of contemporary enterprises" without viewing this as a core contradiction (1999, p. 5). A classic example of this attitude is found in Victoria Marsick and Karen Watkins' chapter in the same book. They spend thirteen pages "envisioning new organizations for learning" and then turn to a number of key criticisms; they do their best to undermine these in a couple of pages without dealing with the key issues raised by the critics before concluding with the desire to create a learning system "tailored to the needs of the industry, the organization, the division, and the individuals who work in this organizational culture" (p. 214)—as if these fundamental criticisms had never been raised and as if all involved share the same "needs"!

Large corporations create hierarchies of control and power and are driven by the profit motive. These control, power, and profit relations create the social relations within work and society. Society's social classes result from these dominant work relations. With the shrinkage of well-paid manual and office jobs—what is described as the "middle class" in North America—society is polarizing into a large working class and relatively small elite. Unless ownership and control changes and becomes genuinely more equitably distributed, nothing fundamentally has changed.

The gap between the richest and the poorest, between those who live full lives in the economically developed countries and those who live "half lives at best" is growing (Honderich, 2002, p. 6). Many workers in Western countries have experienced a decline in the value of real wages, and they must struggle to stay abreast of inflation even at low inflation rates. The fallout from the 2008 global financial crisis and the 2010–12 attack on national debt will ensure that the "social wage" (public services, education, health care, etc.) and public pensions will decline in real terms. The following quote is from *Maclean's* magazine (Canada's oldest current affairs publication and a long-time proponent of free enterprise):

> From 1970 to 1999, the average annual salary in the U.S. rose roughly 10 per cent to US$35,864, says Paul Krugman, a professor at Princeton University. At the same time, the average pay package of Fortune magazine's top 100 CEOs was up an astonishing 2,785

> per cent, to US$37.5 million. "There is no rationale but avarice and greed," says (John) Crispo. "I believe in the pursuit of self-interest, but look at what they do: they rob us blind." (2002, p. 1).[3]

A report by the Canadian Centre for Policy Alternatives points out that in 2011 the top Canadian CEOs made 189 times more than the average Canadian compared to 105 times more in 1998—a huge acceleration in what was already an obscene differential:

> By 12:00 noon January 3 (2012), the first official working day of the year, Canada's Elite 100 CEOs already pocketed $44,366—what it takes the Average Joe an entire year, working full-time, to earn (CCPA, 2012).

WOW

From September 2010 to the same month in 2011 the average earnings of Canadians rose by 1.1% and the top 100 CEOs income rose by 27%. If we add in the other 2,360 Canadians who make up the richest 0.01% of tax filers its clear that those who earn $8 million a year "no longer live in the same world as the rest of us" (CCPA, 2012). But they do have a major say in public policy and spending and suck real resources from the rest of us.

An earlier study by CCPA (Russell & Dufour, 2007) looked at the share of national income going to Canadian workers compared to the share going to profits. The workers' share had dropped from 65.1% of national income in 1978, to just over 60% in 2005; whereas the Canadian corporate profit share of national income had increased from 25.8% in 1978, to 33.68% by 2005. Similar evidence in the US showed workers share of national income down to 51.6% in 2006 (from 59.3% in 1970); and in the UK it was down to 53% in 2009 (from 65% in 1973) reported in a Trade Union Congress report.

How important is this inequality? Sam Pizzigati in *Greed and Good: Understanding and Overcoming the Inequality that Limits our Lives* argues its "the root of what ails us as a nation [referring to the USA], a social cancer that coarsens our culture, endangers our economy, distorts our democracy, even limits our lifespans" (2004, pvii). He argues that CEOs:

---

[3] John Crispo is a retired University of Toronto business professor and outspoken champion of corporate freedom and free trade who has long been associated with the Howe Institute, a private enterprise, think-tank.

> have never (in practice) really accepted the notion that empowering employees makes enterprises effective. Empowering workers, after all, requires that power be shared, and the powerful, in business as elsewhere, seldom enjoy sharing their power. The powerful enjoy sharing rewards even less. Corporate leaders have never accepted, either in theory or practice, the notion that enterprise effectiveness demands some sort of meaningful reward sharing (2004, p. 167).

One of the drivers behind increasing income inequality has been the increasing shift in developed economies away from industrial capital to finance capital that began in the mid to late 1960s. Finance capital had always been attractive; it offered the opportunity to move funds around and make money without the messy business of producing something useful or even offering a real service (jobs in "the city" can be very lucrative without producing anything of worth). However, from the late 1960s large corporations saw the opportunity to move their funds out of manufacturing and into finance (Spencer, 1989, p. 47) and when manufacturing had to take place it increasingly became outsourced. This led to ever-increasing CEO rewards, boosted share prices and reduced wages to workers as well-paid jobs vanished (described as the shrinking of the "middle-class" in the USA). The predominance of a largely unregulated global financial sector—the scale and scope of money capital and financial institutions within the recent period has been termed "financialisation" by Nolan (2011, p. 2) which he argues makes the 2008 financial crisis distinct from previous global economic crisis—also led in most countries to taxpayer bailouts for banks, and bankers, and more loss of jobs for workers.

Neo-liberalism promotes a free market economy approach to social issues, to public provision of services and to public spending generally. It has been referred to as "supply-side economics" and for example rejects the view that governments should try and create more employment directly in favour of a sole focus on the supply of a flexible skilled cheap workforce. The neo-liberal argument is essentially an economic and political philosophy advocating free markets, deregulation, privatization of public assets, more unencumbered free trade, and less government "interference" in economic (and social welfare issues) with the state acting in support of capital.

Neo-liberal economics supports greater freedom and recognition of the captains of corporations but has now become unstuck with the argument that some financial institutions are "too big to fail," which means in effect they are "so big that they can depend on society (that is taxpayers) to prop them up when they topple" (Patel, 2009, p. 19). This is a clear contradiction of the neo-liberal economic arguments of no government interventions in the market. While in theory neo-liberal economic arguments may champion "no government interference," practice can be different.

More severe criticisms of the behaviour of large modern day corporations go beyond the high rates of return demanded of investments and exorbitant executive salaries (sometimes referred to as "greedy capitalism" or noted as a key component of "millennial capitalism") to encompass the exploitation of sweat-shop labour in the "economic south" utilizing "free trade" policies and compliant governments (an aspect of "global capitalism"). Canadian investigative journalist Naomi Klein (2007) has also documented how corporations and Western governments have collaborated to use collective shocks—wars, terrorist attacks, or natural disasters—to push unpopular economic measures (what she has termed "disaster capitalism"). This chimes with John Perkins' (2006) (and other) accounts of the activity of "economic hit-men" who work for global organizations and in collusion with US government departments and international agencies, including the World Bank, to impose loans and economic conditions on debtor countries and gain access to natural resources, and to military and political support along with the countries economic dependency (he refers to these actors in the "modern empire" as a "corporatocracy" p. 255). Klein's and Perkins' concerns also resonate with President Dwight Eisenhower's farewell address in 1961 warning to his "fellow Americans" that:

> In the councils of government, we must guard against the acquisition of unwarranted influence, whether sought or unsought, by the military/industrial complex. The potential for the disastrous rise of misplaced power exists and will persist.

Unfortunately Eisenhower's warning went unheeded and the military/industrial (plus government) complex is now fully entrenched in the US and global economy.

The financial crisis and bail-outs, and the resulting financial hardship for working people, provoked a widespread popular reaction. What the subsequent Occupy Wall Street movement achieved was to focus popular attention on the small elite–the 1%–that benefit from this massive inequality and on the power of corporations to influence public policy (Scipes, 2011). The Occupy Movement has provided the opening for a more thorough discussion of democratic responses.[4]

Reflection on the Perspectives offered in Chapters 1 and 2

There has been an explosion of scholarship in the last fifteen years in relation to workplace learning. Valuable work has been done for example, identifying issues (Bratton et al., 2004) and examining marginalized groups (Mojab & Gorman, 2003; Mirchandani et al., 2008, 2010; Cohen, 2003) and relating these to critical perspectives (Sawchuk, 2008; Sawchuk & Taylor, 2010). Other important work has developed theoretical models of workplace learning (Fenwick, 2006). In many cases, however, workplace learning still remains a list of knowledge issues to be resolved with the hope that "perhaps somewhere can be struck a balance between employees' and employers' interests in creating the goals of workplace learning" (Fenwick, 2006a, p. 195): such views support an HRM unitary perspective on work and learning.

Discussions of workplace learning needs to begin with the substantive issues of equity, power, authority, control, and ownership. These have largely been ignored in the HR corporate perspectives and much of the work and learning literature. We should also acknowledge, too, that much of the mainstream literature is focussed on HRM (and workplace learning) in large organizations and very little has documented work and learning in small workplaces (Delbridge & Keenoy, 2010, p. 805). Large global corporations are important and powerful but they do not employ the majority of working Canadians.

4 Developments in Iceland provide an interesting example, largely ignored by Western media. A referendum determined that the people would not pay the debts created by the banking crisis. Instead, they would arrest the bankers, re-write the constitution using social media, and instruct the government not to comply with IMF requests for cuts in social programs (Stryke, 2011).

Understanding Informal and Non-Formal Learning

The work and learning literature often refers to "informal learning" and sometimes to "non-formal" and "formal" learning and education. These terms need to be explained.

Informal learning can be said to encompass all the learning that occurs when individuals or groups seek to achieve certain objectives. Tough (1979) tended to consider consciously pursued learning projects as more significant than the incidental learning that occurs as a by-product of other activities. Others give more credit to both conscious (explicit) and incidental learning, but discount accidental (incidental and accidental are both deemed tacit) learning (see Livingstone, 1999b, for a discussion of explicit and tacit learning).

But could not all learning that occurs outside structured learning simply be categorized as informal learning? And perhaps how something is learned matters less than what is learned and what results from that learning. At an adult education research conference plenary meeting in 1996, a somewhat exasperated professor of adult education from the University of British Columbia dismissed much of the literature on informal learning as nonsense. His point, it seems, was that lots of people learn lots of things during their lifetime, but so what? Mapping the incidence of adult learning moments tells us little about what they learned and what resulted from that learning. Mapping learning incidents also relies on self-reporting and is subject to suggestion by whoever conducts the survey. Perhaps even more could be made of what is not learned, rather than what is learned, particularly in the realm of ideas and social actions. Absences in knowledge can sometimes be more important than what is known.

Apart from these broader considerations, there remains the question of how to distinguish informal from formal learning. One leading educational researcher gave an example of informal learning taken from his experience as follows. He needed to take a particular course to gain entry to university, so he studied this topic in his own time, at his own pace, and outside an educational institution. But is this informal learning? The curriculum was set, the learner had no say in what was studied, and had to sit an exam and be tested, as opposed to being "tested" by his experience. His purpose was not to advance his general understanding but to gain a credential. Clearly, this is not an example of informal learning but rather of formal learning, albeit in an atypical setting.

Establishing a definition of non-formal learning has also resulted in some problems. The term is not particularly intuitive. Its use in North America and internationally, however, is widespread and causes few problems for experienced adult educators because it can be related to traditional understandings of what adult education is. "Non-formal" refers to not-for-credit courses and educational events that usually take place outside recognized educational institutions and that often have a social as well as an individual purpose. These historic forms of adult education continue in contemporary society.

The differences among these terms —informal, non-formal, and formal learning/education—are certainly not cast in stone. Nonetheless, they are useful categories that make the description of our work in the field easier (for a fuller discussion of these terms, see Selman et al., 1998, pp. 25-26; Spencer, 2006, pp. 9-10).

To summarize the distinctions:

- Formal learning/education carries credentials, has a set curriculum, and is usually provided by an educational institution. In many cases formal post-secondary education is more accurately described as "further" or "higher" education (or generally "post-secondary") and is linked to achieving vocational or academic credentials.
- Non-formal learning/education can be organized by educational or non-educational institutions or by groups or other organizations. It is usually non-credential (essentially non-credit), part-time, delivered via linked weekends, day or week-long schools, and targeted to satisfy individual, recreational or social objectives. It is what we have always understood "adult education" to be. In a workplace setting this could include a couple of half-day sessions learning to use a new computer operating system and figuring out how it would best work at your station.
- Informal learning is the learning that goes on all the time, individually and in groups. It can be conscious (explicit) and/or incidental/accidental (tacit). For example, a worker may learn on the job how to operate a machine, or what is expected at team or union meetings, s/he will learn by observation, participation and through the experience of the work. All these are examples of informal learning.

Putting our three definitions together in the context of this example: the skills, processes, and knowledge gained from general work activity are examples of informal learning. If the workplace offers a couple of half-day training/familiarization sessions on new systems, they are then structuring a non-formal educational/learning event. If a worker signs up for a course or program leading to a professional designation offered by a local college, the employee is entering formal education, usually consisting of credit courses and a credential.

CHAPTER 3

The Learning Organization

This chapter is divided into three sections: a brief examination of groups and teams; a longer discussion of learning organizations; and a discussion of the applicability of the learning organization concept to contingent and precarious work. The chapter also examines the difference between work groups/teams and self-managed teams; and discusses what is implied by "Taylorism."

Groups and Teams

Some form of collaborative work is the norm for most workers. Workers form groups, exchange information, set norms in regard to the work, all as part of the daily routine. Some of these work-groups operate as an interdependent team—for example a "hod-carrier" servicing two or three bricklayers with bricks and mixed mortar; a small finance office that may divide up different inter-linked functions; a fire-fighting crew working with one fire truck; a small group of retail workers stocking shelves in a supermarket at night. For some of these groups/teams the amount of time taken to complete the work, or the pay received, or even their own safety, will depend on how well they work as a team. However, it should always be remembered that for the most part workers are locked into a wage-labour relationship that constrains their group autonomy and influences work-team activity.

The terms "work groups" and "work teams" are often used interchangeably, but they are different ideas. A group of workers may share the same workspace and be able to communicate with one another at different times during the day, whereas a "work team" may be seen as more integrated, sharing tasks, and perhaps rotating and learning each other's "stations" or major areas of responsibility. A "self-managed work team" may get to choose how it does its work and whether or not it wants a team-leader and who it should be. The team is held responsible for completing its tasks and some bonuses may be dependent on group performance.

The growth of factory work, large organizations, and the role of finance created more distance between workers and the end product of their labour. It allowed for more supervision, division of labour, and reduced workers' control over the production process. (Even most sole proprietors in modern economies operate within a nexus of suppliers, distributors, and finance that constrain their own control over their work.) Within larger organizations the impact of these changes was more obvious with work-discipline being imposed—first on the workforce with different shifts, time clocks, and hierarchical supervision and later the work-discipline becoming absorbed by workers (from grade-school on) as part of what "work" means and what "being an employee" means (Curtis, 1988). Of course the ultimate discipline of the employer is never absent; a worker who does not conform can lose their job.

Employers respond to changing circumstances in different ways. For example, a small manufacturer of textiles in Toronto drawing employees from a pool of new immigrant women workers may decide to maintain close supervision to ensure division of labour, individual responsibility, and piecework pay systems: a structure which allows for little genuine group or team work. Whereas an employer working in the digital gaming industry, operating a small office of software engineers, drawing on a more limited professional labour market, may encourage collaboration and team work and pay team bonuses for successful products. However, it is also possible for two different employers in the same industry or service to adhere to two different cultures: one encouraging more autonomous, self-supervising work groups and the other a tightly supervised work culture. Employers also respond to technological changes differently. For example many would find it difficult to resist the opportunity to monitor workers through new forms of technology. They may even break-up a more collaborative and fulfilling service operation just to introduce technological changes that appear to modernize (post-modernize?) and make the processes efficient (Sawchuk, 2010).

From an employer's perspective a self-managed team, assuming it works, can be cost-saving, requiring less supervision and ensuring compliance to team goals via internal group pressure. In some cases this is seen as more effective than management discipline (Bratton, 1992; Wells, 1993). Quite a lot of effort can be expended on trying to find the right number of employees to form a "team" or re-designing work to make teams possible. The Volvo experiment in 1987 was considered the leading example (Bratton et al., 2004, p. 54) in breaking up the Fordist production line into smaller "group technology" or "cell" production (also referred to as "circles" or "islands"—all with the intention of differentiating them from the "production line" beloved by earlier factory design) to allow workers greater flexibility and job enrichment. As noted at the beginning of this chapter, workers do generally enjoy working in groups or teams. Nevertheless, that may not mean they will enjoy the constraints and conditions attached by a particular employer, nor will it mean they will not be aware when they are being exploited. Wells (1993) and Robertson et al. (1989) demonstrated that teamwork could lead to job intensification and speedups, they found that some work teams were being made to work on and meet targets when short-handed and came to see the "team" as primarily a way for management to cut labour costs at their expense.

Job flexibility/job enrichment/multitasking are all terms that have been used to accompany team developments. The idea is that workers will experience more satisfaction in seeing more of the "job" completed, by exercising a range of skills. In completing different tasks to accomplish more of the job, workers are more able to monitor how they are doing in completing their work. On the other hand, while some workers may experience "job enrichment," the extent of "autonomy" and "empowerment" for the team may still be limited.[1]

Learning Organizations

Workplace learning is often presented in straightforward terms: it refers to the learning that takes place at work, learning that workers do on a daily basis. The notion of a "learning organization" extends that simple idea to include a concept of collective (organizational) learning that results from individual or team learning. The idea, thus, becomes more complex, but is still presented as essentially unproblematic: the argument that individuals can "develop" as the organization grows, is essentially presented as a "win-win"

[1] The Hollywood film *Office Space* illustrates a number of different examples of "team" pressure under the new human resource management strategies. For example, the office worker protagonist in the film is expected to be a "team player" and come in to do extra work on weekends (even if it's not needed) at the request of the "team leader" (i.e., supervisor) whenever he is asked (saying "no" is not an option). Whereas his girlfriend in fast-food is chastised for not being a team player for not wearing enough "flair"—buttons with happy faces and messages. Being a good and efficient waitress is not enough. The film is recommended viewing for all those who may have not looked at it as an example of work organization, including the scenes about open plan cubicles and consultants, in the new economy.

situation. Learning in the workplace, it is argued, benefits everyone: an organization may decide to encourage greater decision making at lower levels, workers may choose how to complete their tasks, and worker teams are encouraged: the workers are said to be "empowered" within a "workplace democracy" (Senge, 1990b; Wellins et al., 1991). This enthusiasm is summed up by Senge's (unsubstantiated) claim:

> There has never been a greater need for mastering team learning in organizations than there is today ... if teams learn, they become a microcosm for learning throughout the organization (1990, p. 236).

Some scholarship has however suggested a different understanding based on the idea that there is an underlying tension between work and learning and a broader concept of what lifelong learning could be. These writers maintain there is tension between the imperatives of hierarchical private corporations and societal democratic practice and that has been overlooked (Coffield, 1999).

In addition, research suggests that rhetoric proclaiming the virtues of workplace restructuring (towards cell production, self-managed teams, learning organizations) seldom matches workplace reality in that few organizations actually make such sweeping changes to the nature of work (Bratton, 1999). Bratton's work is important here because he went out looking specifically for international examples of good practice and found few. He approached his study as an academic, not as a consultant–consultants often have a vested interest in the next contract (Senge, 1990; Wellins et al., 1991; Honold, 1991).

Fred Schied and colleagues at Pennsylvania State provide another example of a thorough piece of research on empowerment at work (not using a survey this time but an in-depth case study of workplace change [Schied et al., 1997a, 1997]). His team of researchers found many examples of contradictory outcomes resulting from the application of workplace learning and management reorganization strategies. They also found confirmation of Forrester's fear of how the brave new world in relation to "work and learning" can become part of the new forms of oppression and control in the workplace. They explain how some competent knowledgeable long-time workers found themselves downgraded and left with lower pay. They also demonstrate how "empowered" workers who challenge organizational policies are often quickly silenced (Howell et al., 1996). Other, earlier work questioned whether workers gained more control over work alongside their increased responsibilities (Klein, 1989) and, as noted earlier, demonstrated that teamwork could lead to job intensification and speedups (Robertson et al., 1989).

In those few cases where genuine moves towards a learning organization that includes some benefits for workers have taken place, workers are reported as being better off, as enjoying greater job satisfaction, more flexible work patterns, and having more say over how work is conducted. Bratton (1992) reports that this is often tied to the technological nature of the work (gains for workers are more likely in high-skilled work with batch production favouring a core workforce, but few gains for the less skilled workforce in mass production factories). He also argues that gains are dependent on job redesign as an important part of the organizational strategy, and that such gains are more likely if workers are included in that redesign process (Bratton, 1999). While some of these changes can benefit some workers, often these gains are relatively small not amounting to full "empowerment." As noted in the quote from Keith Forrester above, there can be another side to the "learning organization" story that needs to be taken into account.

In reality there are different interpretations of workplace learning, and organizations are not unitary but pluralist in nature. Researchers need to examine different interests and outcomes that underlay the new forms of workplace learning, particularly in relation to the new forms of global corporations.

Laurie Field (2004), an Australian proponent of organizational learning for ten years, rethought his commitment to the idea. He feels that the weakness in the conception of organizational learning stemmed, first from a confusion and ambiguous use of the terms "organization" and "learning"; second from the focus on "learning associated with technical and economic interests"; and third from the assumption that organizations are unitary (2004, pp. 204-05). He concludes that: "whole organisations rarely learn. A great deal of what has been referred to in the literature as 'organisational learning' is actually learning by shared-interest groups within organisations" (2004, p. 216).

Others have gone further. Mike Welton, a one-time advocate of the value of workplace learning as "development work" (1991), has commented "harnessed to the money-code the business organisation is actually learning disabled. It is intensely pressurised to learn along a single trajectory: to enhance shareholder profits and interests" (2005, p. 100). If Welton's judgment appears harsh, see Perkins (2006) for an insightful insider's view of global corporate behaviour.

A 2007 Conference Board of Canada report suggests the idea of the "learning organization" is on the wane. Canadian companies have moved away from describing themselves as "learning organizations" although the reasons for this change are unknown. It could easily be that the "management fad" has passed and that companies are back to describing themselves as "oil companies" or in "insurance" rather than as "learning organizations." Hughes and Grant, the report's authors, suggest it's more to do with the recognition of what's involved in being a "learning organization" and some companies believe they are not there yet. But the authors have no hard evidence to support this view (2007, p. 2).

Other anecdotal evidence may suggest a decline in organizational learning linked to a focus on short-term profits or simply a failure to retain organizational knowledge as personnel change. For example, a large insurance company cuts a team leader position in a local office as a cost-cutting measure, believing that a self-managed team will simply take over only to find that in a few years most experienced staff become disgruntled and leave, taking their "corporate intellectual capital" with them. Or a high-end real estate developer experiencing employee turnover fails to keep records of standards of service to buyers such as circulating lists of contractors and their contact information, something that was the developer's practice just eight years previously. And also fails to maintain previous contractor supervision practices and then wonders why so many new customers complain about the finishing trades' standards and are disgruntled by the lack of information compared with the developer's experience eight years previous. The developer's "learning organization" had become a "forgetting organization."

Another problem in the HRM (and much of the mainstream work and learning) literature is the tendency to treat all organizations the same, including non-business organizations such as public services, universities, hospitals, non-profit, and non-governmental organizations. All are seen as dealing with "clients" or "customers" within the context of a "business plan" and having to apply business principles to the "bottom line." This can lead to false conclusions. Displacing the principles and standards associated with traditional public sector values and practices will not serve the public interest (Du Gay, 1996b). Scant regard is paid to the notion of the "public good" or the quasi-democratic structures that govern these organizations and distinguish them from corporate environments. Given nurturing circumstances and organizational structures, these organizations may well be capable of more democratic, less hierarchical control involving citizens, workers, their unions, and managers. The workplace "democracy" claimed for corporate learning organizations is never compared to the non-profit sector or worker-owned co-operatives, where workers often participate in major decisions including appointing the CEO and holding him/her accountable to the worker-owners (Salamon, 2003; Martin, 2012).

When considering the workplace as a learning organization it's important to recall the earlier comment–made at the beginning of Chapter 2–that workers have always learned at work; learning at work is not a new phenomenon. Some of what workers learn is useful to the employers, some useful to themselves, some useful to their union organization at work, and some may be useful to both their employer and themselves. Some may have little to do with work itself. It cannot be assumed that all learning at work is translatable into "organizational learning" and is a "win-win" for workers and employers alike. Nor can it be argued this learning always result in "empowerment" for workers; in some circumstances it may result in greater job control for workers, but in others it may result in the reverse.

Being a worker in a "learning organization" is not a guarantee of job security. It may be true that the company's competitive position depends on a more effective and intelligent use of its human resources, but this does not mean that a corporate decision about location or product development will benefit a particular workgroup, or that the rewards from the collective effort will be equitably distributed amongst the workforce.

There is a tendency in the learning organization literature to slip from discussing workplace learning to empowerment to industrial democracy as if they are all one and the same process and, for example, to assume that a statement that a company is "empowering" its workforce means that it is actually happening. Such claims always need to be tested against worker as well as employer experience and situated in a more critical understanding of the "new workplace" and the "knowledge economy."

Taylorism Revisited

Changes at work are often exaggerated to suggest the move from Taylorism to teams and employee empowerment is more advanced than it actually is. Many researchers argue that Taylorist measurement and control at work remains or has been expanded. For example Hennessy and Sawchuk (2003), discuss the deskilling and "industrializing" of frontline social service workers following the introduction of new technology into their jobs. (See also Sawchuk, 2010.) As Tony Brown comments:

> Most descriptions contrast team production to the "scientific management" principles of Taylor. In fact the tendency is in the other direction–to specify every move that a worker makes in much greater detail than before. Management chooses the processes, basic production layout and technologies to be used. Speeding up the pace of work is an intended consequence of standardising production, services or software (Brown, 1999, p. 15).

All of this is made possible by applying new technology into the "new workplace." The appearance of worker control over when and how much work is undertaken is often illusionary, as the new computer-based work comes with constant monitoring and feedback to the employer far exceeding what Taylor was able to do with his stopwatch and clipboard. What we have today could perhaps be described as a more "differentiated Taylorism" or "post-modern Taylorism."

It has also been argued that the knowledge required to successfully engage at work has changed from simple know-how to "work process knowledge." This is a knowledge that "links know-how to theory," a kind of knowledge that was not available in the traditional Taylorist workplace (Boreham et al., 2002). Exactly what this "theory" to be learned is remains unclear. Furthermore, it is unconvincing to argue that workers did not previously possess something akin to work process knowledge (assuming that we can agree on a definition and on its existence–let us assume it implies an understanding of the production process beyond a particular worker's own job), although it might be the case that few of them ever got to apply it. But is the real purpose of "work process knowledge" to turn workers away from understandings of ownership, authority, and control (macro issues), and towards accepting managerial objectives and employer ownership of value added in the production process (micro perspectives)? Such questions are ignored by Boreham and colleagues.

Note that although many authors consider the idea of organizational learning and knowledge work as a relatively new concepts, the ideas have been around in one form or another for some time. Peter Drucker, one of the earliest "management gurus," had a chapter titled "Knowledge is the Business" in his popular 1964 *Managing for Results* text—that is fifty years ago!

We should note that many management ideas are dreamt up by their promoters in the hope that they can top the bestseller list with the "next must-have" management text. This does not always make these ideas poor but what you should be aware of is that few of them are ever thoroughly tested before they are marketed. It is something to look for in reviewing the texts. For example, Senge's *The Fifth Discipline: The Art and Practice of the Learning Organization*, perhaps the most-quoted organizational learning text, makes specific recommendations on how to become a learning organization, but there is no hard evidence that he has identified the key elements. His recommendations are based on his ideas not empirical evidence. A careful reading of the empirical study by Agashae and Bratton (2001) would suggest Senge's model does not work in practice in the way he envisaged it in his book.

Contingent/Precarious Work—The Intersection of Race and Gender

The problems with the "learning organization" model, both theoretically and in practice, are highlighted when we examine the position of marginalized workers, particularly those engaged in contingent work. Mirchandani and colleagues (2010) begin a chapter on "transitioning into precarious work" with the observation that:

> There is emerging evidence that immigrant women of colour are systematically channeled into low-paid and dead-end jobs when they arrive in Canada ... and that several industries depend on highly "flexible," "disposable" and "captive" immigrant women workers for their labour supply ... (p. 231).

Their chapter goes on to examine the experiences of such women. They highlight that many arrive expecting to continue work in the professions they enjoyed prior to emigration to Canada.

The kinds of learning that the women endure includes learning to deal with "unstable, poorly paid jobs" and an ideological or identity shift were women learn to "construct themselves as precarious workers." Immigrant women of colour are clearly a special category of precarious workers but it can be argued that to a greater or lesser extent, all contingent labour has to deal with similar adjustments and undergo similar learning in order to survive.

There is a long history of marginalized labour in Canada. The history of racialization and work in Alberta, for example, has been documented by Kelly and Cui (2012). They comment:

> This systematic racialization of workers, immigration policies, and, ultimately citizenship persisted until the 1967 Immigration Regulation introduced a point "system"—a change agreed to mainly because of the decline of preferred immigrants from northern Europe (p. 268).

They note that although overt racist immigration rules and regulations formally ended in 1967, racialized employment practices persist. The authors go on to discuss the work experiences of different racialized groups including Aboriginal, Chinese, East Asian, and African Diaspora and bring the story up to date with the temporary foreign workers schemes involving Pilipino, Mexican and Central American workers amongst others. There is a long history of racialized labour segmentation that goes beyond the 1967 regulation change, a history that unfortunately chimes with Mirchandani and colleagues' experience in Ontario. Moreover most marginal workers do not enjoy union membership—with the exception of the long history of the Brotherhood of Sleeping Car Porters, Canada's only all-Black union, formed because of their exclusion from "White" rail unions, discussed by Kelly and Cui (2012)—or if they do it is largely ineffective. In the next chapter we will look at workers' learning particularly in a unionized context. The learning opportunities for contingent/precarious workers in work that can lead to promotion and "good" jobs are extremely limited. Companies spend most training dollars on "core" workers, particularly those in managerial and professional grades: those who have most education/training get more.

Society, Workplace Learning and Education

Graham Lowe's (2000) *The Quality of Work: A People-Centred Agenda* and the late Joe Kincheloe's (1999) *How Do We Tell The Workers? The Socioeconomic Foundations of Work and Vocational Education* are very different approaches to resolving the same problematic: how to achieve "good work"—high quality jobs along with enhanced democracy at work and in society. One is Canadian, the other American.

Lowe's study draws on years of surveying the opinions of Canadians on social and economic issues. He found a deep dissatisfaction, not only in the insecurity surrounding employment in the 1990s but also with the nature of work itself. Employees consistently report that they are overqualified for, and their skills and knowledge are underemployed in, jobs they perform. High technology and knowledge jobs are scarce while mundane, repetitive, low paid jobs are commonplace. The study is supplemented by case study data that illustrate workers' experience of the modern workplace. Lowe argues for a balance between work and non-work.

Kincheloe's text is twice the length of Lowe's; it is a denser argument, drawing on diverse sources to support the analysis. He approached the issues as an educator interested in how we should teach about the world of work (what he calls "vocational education"). He addresses questions of diversity in US society and the nature of government, all with a view to contesting the free market claims of corporate America and recapturing what he sees as humane and democratic tradition of US society. He regards the democratic future of the USA as depending upon the democratizing of the work world.

Both researchers demonstrate a good understanding of the contextual issues. For example, they do not reify the learning organization model, they point to examples of bad practice, and of the rhetoric of learning organizations not matching workers' reality. They understand the limitations of corporate self-interest and acknowledge that an active, interventionist, and regulatory role for government can be a positive force. They have a healthy respect for labour unions and advocate (without preaching) a role for unions within the process. They both believe that employers can change and will benefit from democratic change. It is refreshing to read two accounts of work and learning that acknowledge that inequalities of power exist even if they do sometimes suspend this understanding in their enthusiasm for advocating collaboration and change.

Neither author really deals adequately with one of the central contradictions of modern corporations: corporate allegiance to the primacy of shareholders (and CEO) works against social and environmental concerns. Lowe and Kincheloe do shift the focus of workplace learning researchers away from the narrow gaze on isolated workplace change and establish the importance of understanding the large-scale breadth and depth of change needed in work and society relations if any meaningful large-scale change is to occur. The authors establish the need for scholars to grasp the multi/inter/cross-disciplinary nature of the problem under investigation.

Can North America change the way business is done as envisioned by these two authors? Unfortunately, the federal/provincial divide in Canadian politics makes it very difficult to establish a common political environment, even if there was a desire to contest the neoliberal economic agenda (deregulation, privatization, open global markets, minimal government) and the USA shows no signs of adopting a Kincheloe view of the role of government. We will return to what might be needed to change in a "global economy" and at the level of the "firm" in the final chapter.

Labour education & EE development schemes provide the best hope for empowerment for workers & for the democratization of work.

CHAPTER 4

Workers' and Unions' Learning

This chapter opens with a brief discussion of workers' and unions' learning at work, before moving on to a longer exposition of labour education—a key area of work and learning that is under-reported. This is followed by an examination of employee development schemes (EDS). Ideas and concepts discussed in this chapter include understanding unions, types of EDS, empowerment, and an argument for liberal adult education.

Workers' and Unions' Learning at Work

Apart from the obvious day-to-day workplace learning, identifying examples of significant employee-organized learning on the job is problematic. Many situations describing workers undertaking their own workplace learning are more accurately described as responses to manager and supervisor prompting (for example, Honold, 1991). A few studies undertaken from a workers' perspective do throw light on employee knowledge but are often looking at knowledge across the course-training/informal-learning divide which makes it difficult to sort out which examples of "learning" are genuinely worker-initiated rather than union-initiated.

Livingstone and Sawchuk (2004) provide a number of case studies examining learning in different sectors and report on workers knowledge generation within company training courses, union education, and informal workplace and out-of-work situations. While examples of employee-interventions around learning run through the case studies it is not always clear which are employee-initiated. Opportunities may be greater for the auto and small-parts workers than the largely immigrant female garment workers although all may engage in some forms of employee-initiated learning that is both work and non-work related. Issues of control over on-the-job training, pay for knowledge, gender and ethnic divisions, inequitable access to learning, and the struggles of marginalized workers to secure permanent employment have all been documented at different times and are central to understanding what is happening in workplaces. Nor should we underestimate the importance of workers' informal learning and knowledge-sharing as a key component of workplace learning.

Perhaps we should not be surprised to find union-organized learning at work is concerned with broader issues of influence over management policies. An interesting international survey of "employee voice" in six "Anglo-American" countries reports that while workers do engage in learning and knowledge creation activities at work, many would like to have more union representation and more participation in management decision making processes (Freeman, Boxall, & Haynes, 2007). This desire is captured in a quote reproduced in Sawchuk (2001, p. 347):

> As unionists, we have always struggled for a voice. If we have asked for nothing else, we have asked to be heard, to be part of the process. ... Until now, we have been pounding at the door. Asking for an audience ...

This lack of representation and access causes workers to be more guarded and less trustful. The data of Freeman, Boxall, and Haynes, (2007) revealed that those with most access were found to be most loyal.

Another development is the establishment of "union learning representatives" (ULR) and a "union learning fund" in the UK (Shelley & Calveley, 2007). The intention is that ULR will help connect workers to learning opportunities, essentially occupational-related training, and help organize employee learning opportunities. Studies do suggest that in a number of situations these representatives can make a difference, particularly in terms of training opportunities, although it is too early in the process to be definitive. Major questions remain. Is union involvement in new neo-liberal global economic agendas merely incorporation or can unions and ULR moderate the impact of these policies and turn these resources to meet broader social goals? Are ULR worker representatives or are they primarily agents of government and corporate policy? Also do they threaten or do they enhance the tradition of independent union education?

What is known is that after the first four years of ULR only about 10% of workplace representatives bargained about learning provision; the majority adopted a passive administrative role (Kersley et al., 2006, pp. 20, 153). It should also be acknowledged that these developments are taking place at the same time as freely negotiated recognition agreements and collective bargaining structures are being displaced by "partnership agreements" that emphasize employer rights, including in some cases denying the rights of work groups to democratically determine their own union representative (Wray, 2001).

Understanding Unions

This discussion of unions accepts the contradictory nature of unionism (as both a force for opposition and accommodation). There is a tendency towards union incorporation into managerial goals (at both local and national levels of the union) and towards bureaucratization and oligarchic structures and so on. But also independent active unionism may provide the best chance to democratize the corporate workplace (to paraphrase Huge Clegg [1978], collective bargaining is a form of industrial democracy).

With the decline of union influence in many developed economies, other forms of representation, participation, and worker-initiated learning have emerged, bolstered in Europe by EU legislation favouring worker participation, but the results are mixed. "In most cases, employee representatives (in the participatory structures) are merely informed of upcoming changes by management with no input into decision making" (Freeman, Boxall, & Haynes, 2007, p. 177). While implementing new participation and learning organization strategies may be successful in helping employers fight off unions (particularly in the US and the UK), the evidence supports the view that much higher levels of participation is found in organizations that do recognize unions. This would support the view that unionization and employee involvement may be complementary (ibid, p. 196). It is also noteworthy that union membership in the US would treble immediately if workers were free to choose union membership (Freeman, Boxall, & Haynes, 2007).

Labour Education

Labour education refers to education and training offered by labour unions (trade unions) to their members and representatives. The extent to which this education is provided directly by unions or by another agency or educational institution for unions varies from country to country and union to union. A main purpose of labour/ union education is to prepare and train union lay members to play an active role in the union. Another purpose is to educate activists and members about union policy, about changes in the union environment such as new management techniques or changes in labour law. Labour education is also used to develop union consciousness, to build common goals, and to share organizing and campaigning experience. Unions typically have a small full-time staff and therefore rely on what is essentially voluntary activity of their members to be effective at work and in society. The labour education program is thus a major contributor to building an effective volunteer force.

Labour education attracts more participants than any other form of non-vocational non-formal adult education in Western countries and is therefore one of the most important forms of non-formal adult education available to working people. However it is often under-reported and ignored in discussions about adult and workplace learning. The 2003 report on the state of labour education in the US demonstrated that labour education provision had grown since 1968 (the time of the last survey) but that current development was uneven (Byrd & Nissen, 2003). One of the reasons for the lack of knowledge about labour education amongst adult educators in Canada and the US is the division between "labour educators" and "adult educators." Another is that most North American labour education is provided in-house by unions—outside the experience of adult and community educators in the US and Canada.

Most union members learn about the union while on the job (what is often referred to as informal or incidental learning). They probably will learn more and become most active during negotiations, grievances and disputes, but they also learn from union publications and communications, from attending meetings, conferences, and conventions, and from the union's educational programs. Although labour education programs only cater to a small number of representatives in any one year, they are designed to benefit a larger number of members because the course participants are expected to share the learning gained with other union members.

Core Labour Education

Most of the labour education courses provided by unions are tool courses (for example, shop steward training, grievance handling, and health and safety representative courses). The next largest category is issues courses (for example, sexual harassment or racism or new human resource management strategies), which often seek to link workplace and societal issues. A third group of courses can be labelled labour studies, which seek to examine the union context (for example, labour history, economics, and politics).

Tool and issue courses directly prepare members for active roles in the union to become representatives of the union. They are targeted at existing or potential union activists. They are provided directly by the unions, by labour federations or by union centrals (such as the Canadian Labour Congress [CLC], the UK Trade Union Congress [TUC], or the Swedish Confederation of Trade Unions [LO]). Tool courses are also provided for unions by educational institutions (for example by many of the labour studies centres across the US) or by educational institutions collaboratively with the central bodies or individual unions (for example, colleges, universities, and the Workers' Educational Association collaborating with the TUC in Britain). They may also be provided by specialized institutions such as the now defunct Australian Trade Union Training Authority (TUTA) or South Africa's Development Institute for the Training, Support and Education of Labour (Ditsela).

The intention of the dedicated labour studies courses is to supplement trade union tools and issues courses with a broader educational program, and in some cases to provide a research basis for union activity. Some universities have linked directly with unions to offer research collaborations (for example, Leeds in the UK, particularly in the 1970s–1990s, and UCLA in the USA) or to support study and research circles (for example in Sweden). Although unions are usually represented on the "boards of studies" of the university and college offered labour studies programs, they are rarely union-controlled (in contrast to the union-run courses). (The variations in terms of the nature, course structures, and delivery of provision of labour education courses are manifest and this discussion provides but a few examples drawn mainly from Spencer, 2002.)

While tools, issues, and labour studies might describe the majority of labour education, the definitions do not encompass all labour education offerings. Unions are increasingly directly involved in a number of membership education programs, some of which have a "basic educational skills" or vocational purpose. In some cases, union-run literacy and second language courses are tutored by fellow unionists and act as a bridge linking immigrant or illiterate workers to union concerns and publications. Similarly, unions are responsible for a number of worker training programs, which allow the unions to educate workers about union concerns alongside of vocational training. In some countries, skilled and professional unions have a long history of union sponsored vocational training and education courses. Unions, including non-craft unions, are becoming much more proactive in responding to company restructuring and deskilling and are arguing for re-skilling, skills recognition, and skills profiling, as well as challenging employers to live up to their rhetoric on "pay for knowledge." This is a growing area of union educational work and a number of unions in different countries are increasingly becoming more involved in offering general membership education of all kinds (in some cases running courses in basic literacy skills and vocational training jointly with management, for example in UAW and USW plants and schools).

New Developments in Labour Education

Most continuing core labour education is targeted at local union representatives. This important work is ever changing, with differing examples evident in all countries where unions are active. There may be more emphasis on peer tutoring in one country and significant content changes in another. There are particular examples of new specific forms of representative training (such as that for European Works Council representatives in Europe) and examples of union representative training in difficult circumstances (such as those in South Africa where unions are coming to terms with recognition and bargaining after years of opposition under apartheid). We also have reports on more sophisticated educational provision for full-time officers—an under-reported area of representative training.

Training recruiters is another development. The educational components of the US Organizing Institute, the Australia Organising Works, and the UK Organising Academy are important labour education responses to the decline of union influence and to shifting employment patterns. The work undertaken in organizing immigrant workers in Los Angeles is a particular example that has been successful in linking union activity to community groups and community-based organizing, with labour education playing a key role. The Justice for Janitors campaigns have been most impressive and have relied on educational support to bolster activity, recruitment, and contract negotiation—they have also provided a model for similar campaigns in Toronto and elsewhere. The region around LA has bucked the trend in the US, providing a leading example of union growth. Some of this educational and organizing work involves existing union representatives and some of it is targeted at new members and would-be representatives.[1]

In Brazil, Programa Integrar has come to offer relevant vocational training and educational opportunities for the unemployed and the employed. The program illustrates that even in a hostile climate union education can succeed. It provides an example to other countries of how to build community links and to argue for alternative worker co-operative employment for union members in opposition to global corporate power. This example links with others in South America where union members are taking back closed factories and building local economic networks.

Although the use of research circles (workers conducting their own research into workplace or sector problems) has been around for some time, it's clear from Swedish experience that this approach has a bright future in terms of strengthening union activity within the union as well as externally. It represents an important alternative for union members wishing to conduct independent "workplace learning" projects.

Reflections on Union Education

Most of the examples above are in the tradition of independent workers' education. The development of ULR in the UK and the tradition of joint programs (in, for example, the UAW-Chrysler National Training Center and UAW-Ford University) plus others of collaborative union-company schemes point to another direction in workers' education. Many of the joint programs are concerned with employee development in relation to employment, and most are specifically aimed at improving vocational skills. In some cases these programs have been boosted by the desire to develop workers skills in order to remain employed (up-skilling), in others they are designed to provide employment opportunities for workers who have been made redundant. There is of course no guarantee that re-skilling and broader educational upgrading will lead to new jobs. An example of a regional joint union-employer-state program is the Wisconsin Regional Training Partnership, which claims success in both creating new employment opportunities and improvement in

1 Ken Loach's film *Bread and Roses* dramatically presents the story of a group of immigrant labour struggling with the issues as part of the Justice for Janitors campaign.

existing employment (Bernhardt, Dresser, & Rogers, 2004). Another development in the same vein is organized labour's Working for America Institute, labour's nonprofit workforce development initiative. By this initiative, the AFL-CIO hopes, via employer and other partnerships, to boost high skills, knowledge work, and good jobs—the so-called "high road" to future employment opportunities.

Many of the labour education initiatives have elements of both accommodation and resistance to current corporate globalization trends. Some courses and programs can be seen as proactive, others as adaptive, while much of labour education remains reactive (see Spencer, 2002, and the ILO, 2007, for examples). Overall, unions remain an important and positive social organization for working people. The absence of strong independent unions remains a problem for workers throughout most of the world (see the example in the final chapter). Some of the skills-training programs offered through unions may appear to be little different from employer provided schemes. But the thrust of mainstream labour education is towards social purpose and social action. It is aimed at equipping workers with the analytical and organizational knowledge needed to participate democratically in the workplace and society.[2]

Employee Development Schemes

Employee Development Schemes (EDS) that encourage and fund workers to undertake forms of non-vocational adult education of their own choosing have taken root in Britain. The evidence to date suggests that these progressive EDS are benefiting workers in terms of encouraging learning activities (and benefiting employers in terms of worker confidence to take on new responsibilities). While the public policy framework was an important factor, it has arguably been less important than key initiatives undertaken by unions and some employers in promoting these schemes. The early progress on EDS appears to have been spearheaded by Ford and the Ford recognized unions in the private sector and by UNISON (the largest UK public sector union at the time) in the public sector.

As noted earlier, employee development is seen increasingly as an important part of the new HRM. If organizations are to succeed, it is argued, they need to become "learning organizations" and make

---

[2] If you are interested in knowing more about labour education, see *Unions and Learning in a Global Economy*, also published by Thompson Educational Publishing.

better use of their "most valuable asset," human resources; those resources need to be developed via workplace learning, training, and education. Although this new HRM approach finds ready acceptance with many CEOs, it's not at all clear if there is a genuine interest in broadly-based employee development or general agreement on what kinds of employee development should be supported and in particular if non-work related employee development is justified.

From a Canadian perspective, the desire to create a knowledgeable workforce has driven a number of recent Human Resources and Skills Development Canada (HRSDC) policies and Canadian company and union initiatives, sometimes referred to as "work skills" or "essential skills." Developments in other English-speaking countries with similar social and economic frameworks have been of interest to Canadian policy makers. Initiatives in Britain, the European Union, Australia, and New Zealand around issues of training, national vocational qualification schemes, laddering of skills, and other aspects of human resource development have generally been in advance of those in Canada, although a number of initiatives by HRSDC can now be viewed as parallel to these developments. Given this background and perspective, it is important to discover the factors underlying developments in Britain (including European Union membership) and to understand the applicability of EDS to countries such as Canada.

The Union View of EDS

From a union perspective, an EDS is essentially a fund that fully or partially pays the fees of employees who want to take part in education and learning that's not directly job related. In some schemes, paid time off work may also be available. The schemes can fund a range of personal, academic, or leisure interests, including hobbies or sport, opportunities to improve basic skills, or the pursuit of mainstream academic qualifications including college diplomas and university degrees. EDS are seen as helping employees develop their careers or personal interests. The focus may be on broadening workers' transferable skills or simply on encouraging employees to return to learning or develop a learning habit. The union's involvement in negotiating, establishing, and monitoring an EDS is considered essential to achieving these broad goals and meeting union members' learning needs.

The Ford scheme known as the Ford Employee Development and Assistance Programme (Ford EDAP) was set up in 1987 and is generally regarded as the forerunner of private employer EDS. It offers employees the range of personal education and training (non-vocational employee development) opportunities, discussed above, outside working hours. Many activities are offered onsite to fit around shift patterns and have included car maintenance, languages, and keyboard skills, but workers can also go offsite and study a range of adult education programs offered in the community.

A number of other companies have devised their own EDS. EDSs can be grouped into three different categories:

- Single schemes: where one organisation—be it a company, industry, or industry training body—develops its own scheme for its own group of workers (in a company, geographical area, or industry). These borrow from Ford EDAP.
- Coordinated schemes: where several companies work together to set up a co-managed scheme to provide opportunities for all their employees.
- Multi-schemes: where one body, usually the local Learning and Skills Council, helps smaller organisations design their own schemes, and provides them with support perhaps linking them to other small employers' schemes: networked more than coordinated.

The main features of EDS include: access to education and training (not usually job-related); workplace-based (or nearby) provision often delivered by a local college or other educational/training institution; voluntary participation, although participation is encouraged and programs and courses are promoted; learning normally takes place outside of working hours in the workers' own time; employers fund the cost of the learning within an agreed or negotiated range (sometimes expressed as a yearly entitlement and can typically vary between as low as $200 or as high as $2,000 per employee).

Those managing the EDS may negotiate a number of places on a college course or may refund fees for those workers who meet attendance criteria. Some larger employers have developed "learning centres" at the workplace that offer EDS programs alongside the more usual workplace vocational training programs, thus providing a range of opportunities for vocational and personal development.

(Some of this chimes with Canadian professional development (PD) opportunities enjoyed by some workers.)

The benefits for union members include free or reduced cost courses (learning opportunities) that take in the more familiar onsite or close-to-the-workplace locations and are scheduled at times that fit around working hours (including shift patterns). The EDS can offer a "second chance" for members who may have missed out on previous school or college or community learning opportunities. EDS is also seen by unions as offering their members a chance to gain additional, more diverse transferable skills that can offer greater job security, and improved career prospects in the "global knowledge economy marketplace." They also increase self-confidence, morale, and motivation, which can pay off not only at work (and therefore for the employer) but also in increased independent and union activity.

The Impact of EDS

Evidence to date shows that employers who support non-vocational learning can benefit from their modest support for EDS. The learning spills over into increased participation in workplace training, which together with the EDS can provide a more "adaptable and skilled" workforce. The boost in self-confidence, morale and motivation noted above can result in a more positive attitude to training and learning and to a greater commitment to work resulting in lower turnover and absenteeism. The first major study supporting these arguments was conducted on Ford EDAP (Beattie, 1997). It should be noted however that these studies are generally looking to encourage EDS and therefore can be expected to accentuate the positives. The concrete benefits to employers do seem to be real but may also be over-stated.

In Beattie's study, it was found that employees felt better about their work and their employer and returned from their educational activities with greater loyalty and respect for the organization. With the push from EDAP (42% of manual workers took advantage of EDAP), worker involvement in adult education leapt to more than three times the national average for this socio-economic group of adults, a clear benefit for the workers involved. Research has suggested that private sector EDS covered 20% of the private sector workforce (Berry-Loud, Rowe, & Parsons, 2001). This is a significant coverage for schemes that increase payroll costs but are not at first glance financially beneficial to employers. The data provided in this paragraph, particularly Beattie's study, may be interpreted as lending support to the view that EDS operates as a sophisticated and subtle extension of employer control.

Union Action on EDS

Most of the major UK unions have become involved with EDS to a greater or lesser extent. They seek to be a participant from the outset in establishing workplace schemes and regard the most successful as those jointly managed by trade unions and employers. They argue for a commitment to the EDS by senior management and for the learning opportunities to be focussed on what members want, not on business priorities. Unions are well aware of the educational biases favouring the most privileged and therefore argue for the entire workforce to have access to the EDS with a particular emphasis on access for the less privileged. Unions recognize that members will need advice and guidance as to what is available and how to take advantage of the opportunities. All this and course promotion too need to be included within the scheme. In some cases, promotion is shared with the new union learning representatives (Forrester, 2002; 2004).

The leading example of union action on learning is Britain's UNISON Open College concept, which includes labour education, basic skills, return-to-learn, recognition of prior learning, and non-vocational and vocational training opportunities for all union members. This concept connects with members' immediate needs for education and learning opportunities and in time feeds into strengthening union activity and presence in society. It can also provide critical approaches to current issues, something which is lacking from more homogenized adult education and training. UNISON has recognized the failure of much basic adult education to reach workers in the lower socio-economic strata and stepped in with a Return to Learn (R2L) program that provides opportunities for workers to become better educated. Further, they laddered that introductory course up through their Open College to other programs, even to the attainment of full degrees. It takes the "learning society" rhetoric seriously and accesses employer and state funding and claims time-off work for its members. The R2L courses are based on UNISON/ Workers' Educational Association (WEA) developed educational material. Its link with the WEA for tutoring of R2L assures an adult education focus, with materials centred on collective understandings. This educational initiative benefited the members and the union. As a result of increased confidence and understanding gained through the courses, members volunteered for union representative positions and argued for policies to benefit their local membership (Kennedy, 1995). (It should be noted that some of the above has been undermined by legislated ULR and a renewed focus on vocational training along with cuts in WEA funding.)

Other unions have developed these more comprehensive programs as well, linking basic union education to graduate courses for union members focussed on critical social science perspectives but have been stymied by recent economic developments and government policies. It will be interesting to see if "Unite," the newly merged union, can rescue some of the more progressive EDS practices of the former now merged unions (MSF/AMICUS & TGWU).

UNISON's Open College concept has also served as a key example of what unions can achieve in a hostile environment. It was able to sell itself as a major component of the government desired "learning society." Needless to say, the UNISON initiative also served as a good example for other unions (for example, speakers from UNISON have addressed a number of union gatherings in Canada).

A number of reports have been produced in the UK documenting aspects of EDS (Berry-Loud et al., 2001; Lee, 1999; Parson et al., 1998). Two internal assessments, one from the University of Glasgow (Maclachlan, 1999) and the other from the University of Leeds, (University of Leeds, School of Continuing Education, 2001) of the efficacy of EDS at their institutions were influenced by the presence of university adult educators who were able to work closely with on-site unions. It should be noted however that the move to ULR discussed above and the institutionalization of "learning representatives" operating within a state-determined learning framework and union learning fund, may be pushing unions away from the more generic EDS towards narrower job-related training. This has also undermined some of the independence of union schemes such as that of UNISON (and its link with the WEA).

Theoretical Approaches to Empowerment, Workplace Relations, and Learning

Empowerment has become a readily used descriptor of the impact of workplace learning and new human resource management practices. The learning organization is said to empower workers to take control of their own learning and to improve their contribution to company performance. This use of the term empowerment, however, needs to be analyzed more closely. The term is often used to mask the desire to extract more from each employee (this analysis is similar to many others, see, for example, Argyris, 1998). This process, as practiced in many learning organizations, as empowering is somewhat misleading. As Wilkinson has commented, based on his study of the hospitality sector, "empowerment as currently practiced is less empowering than employee participation of earlier times" (1998, p. 49).

Under these circumstances empowerment requires more than a learning opportunity. Workers need considerable resources to challenge such a concentration of power. Unionization needs to be allied to militant union action, employers need to sacrifice substantial areas of control if workers are to be empowered, and eventually workers need to be beneficiaries of any material gains made. It can be argued that union influenced EDS can make small steps towards worker empowerment in a general sense, but in terms of meaningful co-management of the workspace or of society, EDS needs to be part of a more comprehensive union plan for democratization of work and society.

A theoretical approach to understanding workplace relations that makes most sense in English-speaking liberal democracies can be described as pluralist (following Clegg and Flanders, the Oxford School of industrial relations). From this perspective, issues of power, authority, ownership, and control need to be recognized within the workplace (radical pluralists such as Fox would give them more weight and critical writers such as Hyman even more). The framework also recognizes a more sophisticated approach is needed to such issues as "team building," "employee involvement," "empowerment," and other ingredients of the "learning organization." It should be recognized that employers need to give up some control if employees are to gain real empowerment, and that all initiatives cannot be depicted as "win-win." From this perspective human resource development needs to be more holistic and less focussed on narrow vocational training. This theoretical approach can also be viewed as an "adult education" framework (following Lindeman in the US and the "Great Tradition" in the UK and Australia, and early university extension in Canada, with, for example, a focus on liberal humane studies, reflective citizenship, and social purpose) rather than a "human resource management" framework.

Unions may represent a minority of workers in Canada (approximately 25-30% of the workforce is unionized) as they now do in other similar English speaking societies, but their presence in the public sector and large private workplaces offers an important leverage for new ideas around work and learning. Nor should the important role of adult educators be overlooked. The opportunity for employees (manual workers and support staff) to take advantage of EDS in British higher educational institutions owes a great deal to the advocacy of adult educators in those institutions (in addition to the unions and progressive human resource staff and WEA tutors in R2L). Globally, unions, adult educators, and progressive HR staff can act likewise.

This investigation has focussed mainly on UK literature, partly because of the availability of data and partly because of the government support that was given to EDS. (That support in turn helped make data more available—more surveys, reports, etc.) Similar schemes operating under different names can be found in Canadian workplaces, both public and private. In some cases the small amount of funds made available to employees to pursue educational endeavours are limited to "workplace specific" training/knowledge, but in others it can be quite open similar to some discussed above. No survey of Canadian programs has been undertaken and an attempt to obtain a small grant to investigate Canadian schemes was rejected by a committee of the Social Sciences and Humanities Research Council.

Conclusions on EDS

How should we then understand these EDS schemes? They are clearly more than "training"—vocationally linked and limited by employer interests—but much of it is best described as "adult education" in the traditional sense as non-credential, non-vocational education/learning, and therefore part of the "liberal adult education tradition." The majority of EDS cannot be described as "social purpose" adult learning or as "empowering" in themselves. Most of the schemes fall a long way short of the committed education associated with many global labour education programs discussed above.

The case supporting EDS may be argued in terms of the advantages to both employers and workers but it is a mistake to argue that it is best depicted as "learning for and within capitalism" concerned with the "problem of credentializing learning" (Livingstone & Sawchuk, 2004, p. 281). In the case of many union negotiated and provided schemes, EDS is not at all linked to "the problem of credentializing" non-formal or informal workplace learning but to all kinds of non-credential (i.e., non-formal) learning opportunities. In some cases it is linked to collective union education provision that is intended to be empowering. Also adult educators who supported EDS, such as Maclachlan and Forrester, were not naive and were aware that workplace learning misused can lead to increased workplace managerial control. While these schemes are not empowering in the collective solidarity sense that is at times achievable via labour education programs, they can provide a reawakening in individual learning. These schemes can be described as individually empowering and can lead to, and be linked to, more solidarity learning, to other union education, and to independent and union actions, not just to greater employer control.

"Liberal Adult Education"

The argument for liberal adult education for working people, even at a time of crisis, was first made by the UK Ministry of Reconstruction Adult Education final report in 1919:

> We do not wish to underrate the value of increased technical efficiency or the desirability of increasing productivity. But we believe that a short sighted insistence upon these things will defeat its object. We wish to emphasize the need for a great development in non-technical studies, partly because we think that it would assist the growth of a truer conception of technical education but, more especially, because it seems to us vital to provide the fullest opportunities for personal development and for realization of a higher standard of citizenship. (1919 Report quoted in Wiltshire, 1980)

The 1919 Report could perhaps have been forgiven if it had turned its back on liberal adult education (the enormous damage to industry and society caused by the First World War had to be repaired). But the Report's authors recognized the importance of liberal adult education in rebuilding society and called for public funds to be available to support diverse educational providers.

Today the focus is on "education for economy," on training and workplace learning, even more so than in the desperate times of 1919. We have turned our backs on the value of publicly funded "liberal adult education." Is it possible that employee development schemes can provide a way back to the diversified liberal adult education recognized and celebrated in the 1919 Report?

EDS has advantages for ER's & workers
Form of empowerment
increased workplace managerial control
Re-awakening in individual learning

CHAPTER 5

From School to Work ...

This chapter steps back to look at the relationship between work and learning as developed through mass schooling. It starts from the inception of public schools and then moves the discussion forward to review education from the 1930s to the 1990s, followed by a section on neo-conservative re-structuring from the 1990 to the present. It also looks at the concepts of progressive education (including the ideas of John Dewey) and the movement involving "back to basics" accountability and standardized testing. We also examine the different political and sociological ideologies that underpin the arguments that schooling should essentially be preparation for work.

Schooling for Work

As noted previously, early forms of work were rooted in the home and family and learning about work and craft also took place in that environment. Early nineteenth century Canada was characterized by voluntary and informal education. The vast majority of children learned most of what they needed to know from their parents, or from adults in other families to whom they were bound as servants or apprentices. In addition, there were churches, Sunday schools and a few private schools.

Promoters of public schooling (the "common school" movement) had a number of motives for campaigning for public schooling–from basic literacy to Canadianizing immigrants to inculcating morals and religion. But it is important to note that the focus of the school promoters went beyond moral and intellectual improvement–they also sought economic development:

> Canadians, they argued, were too willing to be behind the times. They cared insufficiently about their collective future and seemed to settle for less than equality with their more enterprising neighbours (Prentice, 1977, p. 47).

If Canada was to avoid a second-class position, it was argued, it had to join the commercial race as well as the race for social improvement.

Before European contact, Indigenous peoples also engaged in community and family learning that was crucial to cultural and physical survival. The learning could be considered organic to their way of life or holistic in nature. This was the case until many children were forced into residential mission and/or industrial schools. It was clear that the idea of industrial schools was to prepare indigenous youth for regular, routine employment via attendance and obedience. As the naming of the industrial schools indicates, they were a preparation for manual labour, not for possible professional work (Schissel & Wotherspoon, 2003).

Increasingly over the late ninteenth century, the role of educating children was seen as less that of families and churches, although these remained vital, than of the state, acting through a transformed system of public schools. The schools could now be defined as public institutions in the modern sense of the term, not just because they were publicly financed, but also because they had a public function to perform. There are lots of issues to consider with early schooling, not least the question of how common was the "common school" experience (from the 1820s and 30s and beyond) in Upper Canada (now Ontario). Girls and racial/ethnic groups did not enjoy equal access and working class children generally would have a truncated school experience.

Bruce Curtis (1988) notes that the School Acts of the 1840s and 1850s put new forms of political governance in place. The power of a local school "meeting" to govern its school was severely limited. The direct and regular participation of parents in pedagogical practice was suppressed. Measures were taken to differentiate teachers from the community. The state came to specify the curriculum and the nature of schoolbooks. The direct participatory democracy of communal schooling was replaced by state administration, with limited forms of representative democracy. Although conflicting interests were evident in the construction of the "education state," Curtis points out that this fact does not mean that one class alone made the education state, or that the subordinate classes had no impact.

However, according to Curtis school promoters were attempting to "construct" students into new "political selves"; that is, into citizens and economic subjects who would come to believe the existing political and economic order was natural. The primary aim of schools was not developing literacy, but socializing students into willing supporters of the dominant social and economic structures.

Curtis argued that, although students might feel liberated by their new knowledge, schooling had succeeded in its intended purpose: to teach students to control themselves. New concepts such as "delinquent" and "truant" were invented to signify those who failed to conform, and angry parents found the laws ranged against them when they complained about high-handed teachers and excessive corporal punishment (1988).

It is important to understand, too, that schools were viewed as key instruments for establishing a new ideology and displacing an old one and that is why school reformers took such care over issues of structure, curriculum, and governance. (In this context an ideology can be understood as a set of beliefs and an interpretation of history that supports a dominant group in establishing its view of social policies. If the ideology is accepted and internalized by the subjects they will police it themselves.)

As G. Gutek has argued:

> Since the eighteenth century Enlightenment, individuals and societies have inhabited an ideological world. After the sociopolitical theorists of the Enlightenment and the revolutionaries in the American colonies and in France shattered the absolutist status quo, people first in Western nations and then throughout the world experienced a time during which ideologies originated and then competed for the loyalty of individuals, groups, and nations. With the emergence of nationalism and the rise of modern nation-states, schools were organized to function as constituent parts of national systems of organized education. Further, the rise of social-class consciousness, stimulated by industrialization, also engendered competition between socioeconomic and political groups over the control of nation-states and their governmental and educational systems. As a result, much institutionalized education, or schooling, has been shaped by ideological outlooks and programs (1997, pp. 140–41).

Although schools were not established solely to meet employers' demands to develop a disciplined industrial workforce, they did influence the growth and development of public schooling—influencing its structure, organization, and curriculum. Even later progressive teaching methods can be linked to the desire to teach self-reliance, initiative and problem-solving within a structured environment and therefore in part reacting to changes within the economy.

Education from the 1930s to the 1990s

The debate that took place in the 1930s about the advantages and disadvantages of progressive education provides the basis for more current debates concerning the need for educational change in present-day Canada. The 1930s debate was focussed around the more progressive ideas of John Dewey that came to challenge traditional schooling.

A key battlefield was the school curriculum which was regarded as the primary tool for maintaining stability or for promoting change.

As noted above, the type of school that Egerton Ryerson (the founder of the school system in mid-nineteenth century Ontario and champion of the "common school") established for the masses was designed to instill traditional norms and values, and to teach unquestioning obedience to those in authority. Traditional schooling promoted competitiveness, since that characteristic is essential to success in capitalist society. By the early twentieth century these ideas were being challenged. John Dewey argued that schooling should promote a co-operative rather than competitive spirit and view of society. In Dewey's ideal democracy, people adopt a consistently scientific approach to problems unhampered by the weight of tradition and authority. For Dewey the school itself had to become a "mini democracy"; in a genuinely democratic classroom the teacher must take account of the desires of the students.

Dewey, like Rousseau and other Naturalist philosophers before him, was appalled by the fact that so much of the learning that traditional schooling valued was really quite useless (e.g., memorization, Latin and Greek, mathematical formulas). If schooling was really going to create a better world, then it would have to be of practical relevance, related to the real concerns of the world. Thus, for example, carpentry, cookery, and textile work played a central role in Dewey's curriculum. He argued these vocational activities reflect people's basic need for shelter, food, and clothing; therefore by building a curriculum around these activities one could be sure that learning was always related to basic human needs and concerns.

These practical activities were not seen as an end, but rather as a starting point. Dewey believed that education needed to be based on experience—the interaction of the person with the environment. This education he likened to the scientific method and was labelled "experimentalism."

Thus to sum up the Philosophy of the Progressives influenced by Dewey:

- The main point of education is to make society more democratic. This goal means fostering more shared interests that bind people together, making them more co-operative and making them more scientifically minded in their approach to problems.
- Students are to be given much greater freedom in the classroom. In this way, they are prepared for the responsibilities of participating in a "free" society.
- The curriculum is to be organized around occupations—vocational type activities. In this way education is to be made relevant to the everyday concerns of students.
- As far as possible a child's learning should be self-directed. Learning is a matter of independent problem solving.

This is what the progressive and controversial philosophy of child-centred and experimental education was based on. Educational philosophies emerge and retreat according to the economic and social climate of a specific historical period. So it was that progressivism, as a social philosophy underlying child-centred approaches to education, dominated educational debates not only in the 1930s but also in the 1960s. Although neo-conservatives blame progressivism and child-centred education for many, if not all of the social and moral ills of the present education system, when classroom practices are analyzed, very few are organized in a manner that can be described as essentially child-centred or progressive. In addition the vocational elements of Dewey's thought can be used to support a criticism that this type of schooling also "sorts and sifts" students into particular vocational streams. In spite of these limitations the criticisms of a child-centred curriculum have been used to advance an even greater focus on preparing students for the work world by advocating a return to traditional schooling's emphasis on the "basic skills" and a teacher-centred presentation of knowledge (with of course the teacher following a determined official curriculum).

The Hidden Curriculum

For some critics of the way in which schools prepare children for the discipline of work, the "hidden curriculum" is as important, if not more important, than the official curriculum. The "hidden curriculum" is a term used to describe the unofficial "3Rs" of Rules, Routines, and Regulations that must be learned by pupils in order to survive comfortably in most classrooms (Jackson, 1968). Pupils must also learn to cope with "delay, denial and interruptions that accompany learning experiences in schools." (Meighan, 1981, p. 58)

Besides academic subjects and explicitly taught curricula, there is a set of norms, attitudes, and values or principles that is implicitly conveyed to pupils by teachers. This hidden curriculum is believed to promote social control at school and in society at large by training people to conform to the status quo. For theorists such as LeCompte (1978), and Bowles and Gintis (1976), these norms and values both reproduce and correspond to the norms and values of the working environment that the students will enter after school. LeCompte identifies the following aspects of the hidden curriculum that are stressed in school: authority, timekeeping, work, achievement, and order. The hidden curriculum can also operate in spatial arrangements of the classroom. Note the following comment by Herbert Kohl (1970, cited in Meighan, 1981, p. 65):

> the placement of objects in rooms is not arbitrary and rooms represent in physical form the spirit and souls of places and institutions. A teacher's room tells us something about who he is and a great deal about what he is doing.

The use of the word "hidden" can cause problems when we try to conceptualize how the "hidden curriculum" is applied in the classroom. Meighan (1981, p. 54) asks whether it is hidden intentionally to manipulate and persuade, or because nobody notices or recognizes it, or because it has been forgotten or neglected?

There is questionable evidence of the extent to which Canadian schools ever became "child-centred" in a truly progressive manner. In any case, the kind of schooling that emerged after the progressive debates in the 1930s and again in the 1960s remained concerned to meet the demands of the workplace. An emphasis on preparing students vocationally together with the persistence of the disciplines of the hidden curriculum contributed towards providing a compliant and prepared new workforce (Contenta, 1993).

Neo-conservative Re-structuring from the 1990s

Arguments for neo-conservative re-structuring of the education system emerged in the late 1980s and the 1990s and continues today, as a response to demands for a more "economically relevant" school curriculum. The neo-conservative reform movement, including its focus on testing, charter schools, and private schools draws on writings by Andrew Nikiforuk (1993) *School's Out: The Catastrophe in Public Education and What We Can Do About It* and Joe Freedman (1995) *The Charter School Idea: Breaking Educational Gridlock*. These texts were contested by authors such as Maude Barlow and Heather-Jane Robertson (1994) *Class Warfare: The Assault on Canada's Schools*, who write in defence of existing public school provision.

During the 1980s, neo-liberal ideology grew in strength. Governments in North America, Europe, and New Zealand adopted an approach to the public sector that emphasized minimum government (cutting in the public sector) combined with tight central control over the remainder of public services. The purpose of government and public services was shifted away from ideas of public provision of public goods towards an emphasis on market solutions to public service issues. As a result, privatization of public services was rampant. Governments introduced fiscal constraints that resulted in a decline in the funds channeled into public education and moved the costs of further and higher education from the public purse to the individual student. Neo-conservatives added to the neo-liberal economic arguments by emphasizing discipline, order, and respect for authority plus a moral code of ethics and behaviour (usually invoking Christianity).[1]

These cuts were combined with an argument that public education was failing to teach the basics and prepare individuals for work. It was also argued that education was pushing liberal (meaning in this case diverse and relativist) and social ideas (meaning "socialist" for some protagonists), at the expense of classical liberal and traditional individual values, and therefore needed to change direction. The arguments in favour of educational changes began in the United

---

1 Neo-conservative is the term used in much of the early educational literature but has been replaced by neo-liberal in more recent writing. We will use both terms as appropriate but recognize they are now generally considered as interchangeable. The other use of neo-conservative is in relation to US foreign policy, for example "GW Bush and his neo-conservative (neo-con) administration."

States with texts such as Allan Bloom's *The Closing of the American Mind* (1987), which laid society's ills on the softness of the so-called "free-spending 1960s" and on progressive educational ideas which, Bloom argued, undermined "Americans sense of intellectual and moral judgment" (Gutek, 1997, p. 289). (For a defence of public schooling, see Friesen & Friesen, 2001: Robertson, 2007.)

Political and Sociological Ideologies

During the early 1960s and '70s the dominant political ideology could be described as liberal reformism (a combination of individualism and social welfare). Public education was part of the welfare state, but it came primarily to be regarded as a tool that could link "fairer [i.e., less class-based] selection procedures to the 'manpower' needs of a technologically expanding society" (Erwin & MacLennan, 1994, p. 2). Liberal ideology—supported by the ideas of functionalist sociologists such as Talcott Parsons—promoted schools as a rational, efficient means of selecting and sorting students for the future workforce. Those with most talent would rise to the top and move into key jobs—jobs that would sustain a modern society. Society was seen as a meritocracy that functioned in the interests of all (a view that downplays the importance of social welfare and equity).

In addition to the social cohesion aspects of functionalism, the functionalist argues that the major basis for individual student advancement towards more highly valued roles within society is via individual achievement. It is assumed that this individual striving serves society's needs, that society continually evolves (for the benefit of all), and that this evolution necessitates higher levels of education and training. Hence, in functionalist theory, society is generally considered both meritocratic and technocratic. As society evolves to a more advanced technological form, formal education is seen as an increasingly important element. From an individual's perspective this can be illustrated by the creeping credentialism that is affecting well-paid employment opportunities; it is almost impossible to find a "good job" (a job with good pay and benefits, prospects for promotion, etc.) without a good education.

It is important to recognize some of the limitations of this functional analysis. First, there is no guarantee that progressive societal developments will benefit the majority in an equitable fashion—they may simply favour the rich and powerful. Second, what appears to be merit may in fact be a reflection of privileged opportunities being masked by educational credentials. In practice most students who do well come from upper and middle class homes. (They have "cultural capital" which allows them to do well in school.) Also, while some individuals may succeed in progressing through the social system via educational qualifications, many other talented individuals may be sufficiently disadvantaged, by a combination of such factors as social class, race, or gender, to be unable to progress. Finally, it can be argued that to the extent that a meritocratic educational system is successful in providing opportunities for some individuals, it basically leaves the existing social system intact, ensuring that the mass of the population will not progress.

In spite of these limitations, it should be noted that liberal reformist policies, although essentially politically conservative, were different from the new neo-conservative ideology. Neo-conservatives/neo-liberals are generally not interested in equality of educational opportunity and the broader liberal curriculum; they are much more focussed on a vocationally relevant curriculum (with less time for traditional liberal and social studies), and wish to introduce market forces into the funding of education and into the curriculum.

Another major influence on education from the sixties has been the development of human capital theory as discussed earlier. In the eighties, human capital theory was revised and individualized alongside the rise in neo-liberal ideology: now it was the individuals' responsibility to raise their own "human capital" to make themselves more employable. In addition, public education (particularly post-secondary) was to be charged more against the individual student, and was to be more focussed on meeting business needs. Education was still seen as an investment, but now it was not so much society's investment as that of the individual. However, a role for the state was maintained in the idea that if a society was to prosper it needed a well-educated workforce ready to meet the challenges of a "knowledge-based economy."

No matter how you interpret human capital theory, it is important to recognize that it is an argument favouring "education for economy"; that is, it views the central purpose of education as being to serve the economic needs of society. As a theory it has proved pervasive and has influenced educational developments in Canada and abroad.

Neo-conservative Ideology

The term "neo-conservative" is essentially interchangeable with "new right," "Post-Fordist," or "neo-liberal" in the sense it is used here. In their book *Sociology of Education in Canada* (1994, pp. 16–18) Erwin and MacLennan identify three elements to neo-conservative ideology:

- "Fiscal retrenchment," summed up in the phrase "fewer programs, fewer people." Governments should do less, and employ fewer people doing it.
- A "claim that the liberal and social democratic policies of the sixties and the early seventies have led to a decline in intellectual standards" in schools and universities. The neo-conservative response to this postulated decline has been an advocacy of "back to the basics" in educational institutions, stressing language arts and math and the vocational relevancy of the curriculum.
- There is an increasing demand that schools and universities be subject to market forces and mimic corporate management techniques.

In addition four main changes in the organization and management of education are seen by Erwin and MacLennan (1994, p. 18) as necessary to ensure the success of this neo-conservative agenda:

- "The imposition of top-down educational management and the use of quantitative indices of efficiencies" and performance (such as standardized testing).
- "Support for parental choice in education" through the privatization of public schooling. Privatization could be direct, or could occur through the establishing of a school voucher or coupon system (summed up by the phrase "the funding follows the student" rather than goes straight to the institution).
- "Encouraging greater responsiveness in universities to corporate research agendas" and encouraging partnerships in research.
- "The introduction of centralized state control over education" to guarantee that schools are "responsive to anticipated labour market" trends. (This centralization is contradictory to the belief in free market forces, but its purpose is to

ensure a minimum level of socialization and training for the mass, while retaining choice for the few. It also has the effect of bypassing local school-board democracy, which might thwart the neo-conservative agenda.)

In essence the term "back to basics" implies:

> "a return to a traditional curriculum and teaching styles" along with "standardized testing" a curriculum with "closer links between what schools teach and what employers want" (Erwin & MacLennan, 1994, p. 17).

Accountability—Standardized Testing

The neo-conservative reform movement advocates standardized testing as an external measure of teacher and school performance, and of how effective educators are at teaching the curriculum. Linked to standardized testing is the further issue of the publication of school test results.

The rationale for the publication of test results is that education should be treated as a commodity in a "free-market" economy, a commodity that will thrive or wither according to public demand. Therefore parents need to know which schools are successful and which are not. The neo-conservative expectation is that schools that are seen as operating efficiently and effectively will attract more students and therefore more funding, and that student test results provide a measure of efficiency and effectiveness.

Test results become the surrogate for "standards," and are used to hold teachers and schools accountable. It is far easier to cite test results, uncluttered by any considerations of social inequality, as a measure of school success or failure, than to deal with the complex issues of standards and equity:

> Policymakers are well aware of the high symbolic value that tests and test results can have in creating an image of [educational] progress or reform. By mandating a test, policymakers are seen to be addressing critical reform issues forcefully, in a way the public understands. ... It offers the appearance of a solution, and is believed by policymakers and the public to be a true solution (Madaus, 1988, quoted in Murphy, 1994, p. 248).

Standardized testing, therefore, appears to be designed to convey the message that something is being done. A league table of school results makes good press copy, and allows parents to compare their child's school with others. Test results also allow parents to compare their child's individual performance with that of the "average" child. As a result, testing to monitor and enforce standards is a major political issue as reflected in the School Achievement Indicators Project (SAIP) testing program sponsored by the Council of Ministers of Education. However, Barlow and Robertson (1994, p. 118) note, a Decima poll taken shortly before the announcement of the SAIP program "found no evidence of a groundswell of public demand for standardized testing or widespread concern about accountability": it would appear that public support for testing had been manufactured. As two commentators for the Canadian Education Association remark:

> We must also question the efficacy of the efforts of some corporations, and in some instances, governments, to convince Canadians, such as those in this poll, that we indeed do have problems that could affect our productivity and world economic position in the future. ... If there is a problem, and the authors believe there is, then other methods of mobilizing the Canadian public to be concerned about this matter has to be considered (Quoted in Barlow & Robertson, p. 118).

In spite of these concerns, however, testing is politically attractive because testing is seen as objective. Therefore, anyone who objects to testing–a neutral, objective measure–can be depicted as politically motivated. Testing does measure an individual performance at the time the test was administered. However, what it measures is what the testers agreed to measure. Some questions may be chosen more because they achieve a spread of responses than they are a good test of knowledge. Furthermore, even if we assumed that the best possible test was administered in the best possible conditions, we must still account for a host of social and educational factors that may affect test results. For example, a good result for an individual may reflect good coaching for the test, or good overall teaching, or a good performance by a bright socially advantaged child performing well on a particular day, or a combination of these factors. A good result for a school may have more to do with the social composition of the school's pupils than with good teaching. A poor result may reflect a less socially and educationally advantaged school population, rather than school performance.

However, we should not overlook the appeal of dominant discourses, and the insidious way in which they become absorbed in "common sense" understandings of the real world. As Mitchell (2003) puts it,

> those pushing a neo-liberal agenda in education stress ... the necessity for greater ... accountability and the imperative to create hierarchically conditioned, globally oriented state subjects–i.e. individuals oriented to excel in ever transforming situations of global competition, either as workers, managers or entrepreneurs (p. 388).

Learning to Labour

What underscores all of these arguments in favour of "back to basics," testing, charter, and private schools is a view of schooling as essentially preparation for work. The idea that the purpose of education is to fulfil broader social goals and provide individuals with a more liberal pluralist perspective on society is relegated behind an argument that favours the primary purpose of schooling being to prepare young people for the world of work and education should be restructured to meet that primary goal (inclusive of a moral education).

While promoting a broader conception of educational purpose and not accepting the view that the only goal of education is to prepare students for work many commentators accept that is one of the educational goals, "[i]t is widely accepted that a major purpose of schooling is to prepare people for work" (Wotherspoon, 2009, p. 179) both in terms of skills, knowledge and credentials and in terms of attitudes and behaviours considered necessary for competition in a globalized economy (and it is also part of the hidden curriculum). There are a number of studies looking at the transition process from school to work that are focussed on the last years of compulsory schooling and the role of "shop" education as well as entry into apprenticeships and apprenticeship experience (see for example "Building a future for high school students in trades" by Taylor & Watt-Malcolm, 2008).

Paul Willis and "Learning to Labour"

Before moving on, we should acknowledge the longevity of the work of Paul Willis' *Learning to Labour* (1977). Willis investigated the lives of mainly white working class male youths in a West Midlands town in the UK tracking how school and social life was preparing them for identifying with a life of limited job opportunities as "labourers" or "manual workers." The study took the ideas of the hidden curriculum and the underlying theme of education as preparation for work and combined it with Willis' ethnographic methodology and sociological/cultural studies gaze. Even the resistance to school life by some of the rebels could be likened, he argued, to the "workplace resistance" behaviours found in some workers in local industries.

Although such students exhibit human "agency" in making choices, for many it is within a framework of what is most available and common within their social/group/family experience. They choose an identity shaped by the schooling "ideology"—a "political self"—bounded by class possibilities and limited horizons. It is worth noting that some of this framework has changed. Following a conference celebrating this work's twenty-fifth anniversary, Jennifer Logue and Cameron McCarthy commented on the studies of Black youth in Alberta by Jennifer Kelly (2004):

> Paul Willis's nationally and geographically inscribed "lads" are now being replaced by Jenny Kelly's Afro-Canadian youth who are patching together their identities from the surfeit of signs and symbols that are crossing the border in electronic relays of US television, popular music, and cyber culture (2007, p. 19).

This "borrowed identity" is also experienced within a school context that regularly encourages sports or arts and crafts rather than academics for African-Canadians—hence preparation for manual work not for professions.

CHAPTER 6

... And Workplace Learning to School

This chapter begins with a discussion of an example of the use of prior learning assessment and recognition (PLAR) and then reviews what PLAR is. This review leads into a discussion of adult learning and the meaning of knowledge. Some of the problems with PLAR and credentialism are discussed next. These issues are usually ignored in discussions of PLAR. We also explain the difference between critical thinking and critical thought and whether or not PLAR increases access to higher education. The section on workplace learning and PLAR argues that PLAR is an important component of the work and learning debate both at work and in post-secondary institutions (further and higher education) and recognizes that mature student entry and the recognition of experiential learning will have an effect on those educational institutions that are open to these arguments. The chapter concludes the PLAR debate by making the case for a sensitive, less vitriolic, discourse on the limits and possibilities of PLAR. The final section takes a brief look at work and learning in the academy itself—under the influence of the neo-liberal agenda—and discusses the concept of the corporate university.

An Example of the Use of PLAR

DaimlerChrysler decided that all higher-level supervisors and administrators in their Canadian plants would in future hold a university degree. They noted that the majority of the existing staff did not have a first degree and set about arranging for them to gain one. They linked up with Humber College and with what was then British Columbia's Open University (BCOU) to grant credit for prior learning, including learning gained on company courses, and to provide a few credit courses. BCOU provided two capping courses and awarded the degree. This "120-credit degree" (four year) could regularly be achieved with just five three-credit college courses and in some cases as few as the two BCOU courses in addition to the supervisors' prior learning and transfer credit of company courses (Meen, 1999).

The presentation of the DaimlerChrysler scheme to a PLAR conference brought forth gasps of admiration from much of the audience for the revolutionary approach. But more cautious attendees wondered exactly what it was that these workers had achieved. Was the BA General degree from BCOU really equivalent to a four-year degree? Had the "students" had the opportunity to investigate significant areas of knowledge, or to interrogate ideas, arguments, and their own assumptions and prejudices in the same way as mainstream undergraduates? (This is not to argue that all traditional students accept the opportunity.) Why did the company not re-think its proposed change? If a majority of staff did not have a first degree but were performing at an acceptable level then perhaps a degree was not needed–why crank up the credential requirement? Perhaps what the company should have done is identify those attributes that lead to success in the supervisory and administrative positions and then consider how to assess those for existing workers and develop workplace learning and courses to achieve the desired outcomes for those who did not have them.

This example–confusing the work-based learning with university education, and with PLAR processes to gain a credential–underlines some of the complex issues discussed in this chapter.

Prior Learning Assessment and Recognition (PLAR)

No one reading the adult education and work and learning literature can be unaware of the emphasis that is being placed on learning at work. Alongside this new emphasis is a demand that learning at work be recognized within the traditional educational institutions when learners seek to make the transition to formal education and training in colleges and universities. As more and more college and universities institute prior learning assessment and recognition (PLAR) programs, educators are increasingly confronted by the question of how to fairly and accurately assess the educational merit of informal learning and non-formal adult education and training.

PLAR is the preferred term in Canada, others include: prior learning assessment (PLA); accrediting prior learning/assessing prior learning (APL); accrediting experiential prior learning/assessing prior experiential learning (AEPL/APEL); and recognition of prior learning (RPL). Although APL is sometimes reserved for transferring previous course learning, and differentiated from AEPL/APEL, PLAR will be used in this discussion to represent all of these terms. The promotion of PLAR is at times almost "evangelical" with a "you're either with us or you're against us" attitude displayed by some advocates. PLAR has become a worldwide "movement" encompassing Australia/NZ, Southern Africa, Europe, and North America with an International Consortium for Experiential Learning established after a conference in London in 1987. It attracts radicals who see PLAR as important for increasing access for previously disadvantaged groups and as a way to open up stuffy universities (Thomas, 1998; Peters, 2001; Andersson & Harris, 2006) but also attracts politicians and business leaders which suggests they may well view PLAR as a mechanism that will help them turn traditional higher education towards meeting the needs, priorities, and interests of the "real" world as they define it: that is the interests of corporations and global capital. Adult educators have always valued student experience in the classroom and while there is broad support for PLAR for adult students, there are also a number of concerns, such as those about PLAR processes, the transferability of knowledge, and dilution of the critical, social, emancipatory purposes of education.

There are a number of ways of assessing prior learning; these include challenge exams, portfolio assessment (perhaps the most common), and demonstrations of skills and knowledge. Transfer credit is not included here since this essentially refers to the transferring of credit gained from one institution's courses to courses and programs of another. The essence of PLAR is the recognition of non-course learning gained experientially, perhaps as a consequence of family, volunteer, or workplace activities or private self-guided study. PLAR can also include recognizing learning in non-formal adult courses including company training that is ascribed credit. There are perhaps three basic assumptions behind the PLAR movement according to Human Resources and Skills Development Canada:

- significant learning can and does take place outside the classroom;
- it should be evaluated for credit by educational institutions and by the workplace for hiring and promotion; and
- education and training practices that force adults to repeat learning are inefficient, costly, and unnecessary (HRSDC, 2007, p. 1).

The process of completing a portfolio is represented as educational in itself, helping students to reflect on experience, gain confidence, and redefine goals (European Commission, 2002; Peters, Pokorny, & Sheibani, 1999). The preparation of a portfolio takes time but it generally takes considerably less time than studying the courses for which PLAR credit is given. Similarly while the new knowledge explored via reflecting upon experience may be significant, it is probably less than the new knowledge available from taking the credit equivalent courses. It also should be acknowledged that assessing portfolios is problematic and the credit awarded often hinges on the student's writing skills as well as their ability to translate experience into "learning." Many institutions are now offering a "PLAR portfolio" course to aid students in the writing of the portfolio—the students get credit for undertaking the course and submit the completed portfolio for additional credit.

The process of PLAR is most often presented as theoretically unproblematic: the vast majority of research focuses on the technical questions of how to measure learning's worth and also how to persuade traditional educational institutions, and "elitist" academics, to accept PLAR credits (Thomas, 1998; European Commission, 2002; Peters, 2001). The case for PLAR fits best with technical training programs that have identifiable skills and abilities as the course objectives (outcomes). Behavioural learning theories that emphasize "competencies" or "learning outcomes" best fit with this instrumental approach to training. Students are encouraged to match their skills to the course outline and outcomes and claim the credits. PLAR can also be useful for workers to demonstrate they have knowledge and skills that are needed for promotions or PLAR can be applied to "laddered" skills-based job categories (for example, as used in Australia).

PLAR meets most opposition as a method of gaining credit within academic programs (particularly in those programs that are not professional or applied); most courses in traditional academic programs are presented as non-instrumental since the knowledge areas, theories, and learning processes of critical reading and writing they concentrate on are outside of, or beyond, common discourse. Where PLAR is applicable to these programs it is often easier to grant generic course credits that match up with the broad program goals, similar to French practice, than to grant specific course credits (European Commission, 2002). (Mature student entry to academic programs has been around for some time and is generally a less contested use of PLAR.)

Credentialism, Adult Learning, and Knowledge

At the core of many PLAR problems is a central contradiction of formal education that is writ even larger when considering experiential learning. One aim of education is knowledge exploration and creation; the gaining of insights and understandings (in short, learning) but the outcome and importance of formal education is increasingly seen as the credential. As a result many learners (and educators) substitute the credential for learning as their central objective. For those seeking PLAR credit, recognition can become the only goal. Instead of using PLAR to focus attention on the gaps in skills or knowledge (what is yet to be learned) the emphasis is placed on finding the fastest route to gain a credential (how many courses can the student bypass and how many does the student have to do?).

For example, if it can be demonstrated that a student has knowledge of 60% of a course curriculum, the PLAR advocate will argue they should be given the credit (i.e., treated as a "pass"). An instructor who responds by suggesting they should study the areas about which they have no demonstrated knowledge (the other 40%) is likely to be dismissed as applying "double standards," for is it not the case that their students can pass with 60%? There are lots of issues here, ranging from the question of whether the applicant has 100% knowledge of the 60% claimed, to the minutia of how specific instructors grade and assess course content (for example, many instructors set assignments to sample from all sections of the course and require a "pass" in all sections) to the bigger questions of what is the purpose of course evaluation and grades and what are they measuring?

Adults learn for a whole variety of reasons and in a complex web of settings. The purposes of such learning may be communal or social as much as personal. Adult learning is in danger of being coopted into a corporate view of what is measurable, exchangeable, and credit-worthy; the complexities and nuances of learning itself may be corrupted by ingenuous and largely instrumental PLAR processes. The question of how or if PLAR processes can be used to promote and foster emancipatory and democratic educational practices in an increasingly credential obsessed "learning society" has been largely ignored. The argument for PLAR also raises the question of whether all adult learning should be viewed in terms of what is measurable, exchangeable, and credit-worthy. For example Derek Briton has argued that the "use value" of certain knowledge is being confused with its "exchange value," what is very useful in one situation may not be "exchangeable" into course credits (Briton et al., 1998). It also "undervalues" experiential learning that cannot be transferred. This is not to claim that one kind of knowledge is superior to the other, but rather that it is simply different and serves different purposes. When an individual decides they need to know more about a certain topic in order to solve a particular problem at work, they are unlikely to be focused on developing critical reading and writing skills. In most cases they are not going to seek out differing perspectives on a problem and then write an assessment of the various arguments. Experiential learning can be useful when undertaking course-based learning, but it may be quite legitimate to argue that the prior learning is sufficiently different that it cannot be credited as if the applicant had undertaken the course of study. In these situations accelerated courses suited to mature adults may be most useful (for example, many individualized distance education programs allow for student self-pacing and for students to draw on prior knowledge).

PLAR emphasizes specific and generic skills as the "outcomes" of learning rather than the gaining of insights and theoretical understandings around a particular area of knowledge. But the transference gained through PLAR into academic (as opposed to applied) credits is mainly based on what knowledge has been gained. Amongst adult education scholars the usual starting point for a discussion about knowledge is Habermas (1972)—for example as used by Mezirow in his theory of perspective transformation (1981). Habermas considers knowledge as the foundation of culture and identifies three forms of knowledge growing out of human activity and interests in work, in communication, and in freedom of thought (linked to an understanding of unequal distribution of power and the role of ideology). Habermas' model recognizes the importance of beginning with an empirical-analytic framework and of moving beyond that to transforming and liberating the consciousness, hence the importance of critical social sciences (Waters, 1994). It's clear that using this framework would lead to an understanding that knowledge gained through work could be limiting. However, claims have been made about new forms of work requiring new forms of knowledge (discussed earlier in this text) and that corporations are looking for "critical thinkers" in their organizations (Boreham et al., 2002). Such claims have to be balanced with an understanding of how firms, as argued earlier, want new recruits to be "on the same page" prior to in-house training and how the "leader's" or "coach's" (i.e., manager's) job is to "help people restructure their views of reality" (Senge, 1990b).

We also need to note a distinction between "critical thinking skills" and "critical thought" (for example, as promoted in critical theory). Critical thinking implies such important abilities as recognizing faulty arguments, or generalizations and assertions lacking evidence, or truths based on unreliable authority (its often represented as an ability to "problem solve") but it does not necessarily imply critically examining life itself or an examination of power and authority or the role of ideology. Whereas critical thought, according to critical theorists, begins by questioning belief systems and by asking who benefits from dominant ideas, its project is educational and emancipatory (Burbules & Berk, 1999). Some authors may claim these two overlap and it is not difficult to imagine a situation in which a critical thinker also becomes self-analytical and reflective about the origins of belief systems. (Brookfield's 1987 text can be read in this way.) But it is difficult to imagine how a critical thinker who has become a critical theorist can be welcomed in many of our modern-day global corporations with their focussed global objectives and narrow practices that demand loyalty and punish criticism (Klein, 2000). (See Brookfield's 2005 text for a fuller discussion.)

Adult educators have always acknowledged the importance of adult experience in the classroom (Knowles is just one example) but knowledge gained through experience is not unproblematic. For example, Freire's work has been used to justify the idea that peoples' knowledge is unrecognized and unacknowledged in the academy and it is about time the knowledge gained through work was formally recognized by the granting of university credits (repeatedly claimed by presenters at Canadian PLAR Conferences, 1998; 1999). But this reading of Freire ignores his understanding that experience was only a starting place, and could be very limiting leading to a "culture of silence." His argument is for a dialogical and collective education that results in workers "renaming" the world they occupy and eventually organizing to change it (Freire, 1970). His concern with self-awareness, action, and reflection is similar to Feminist scholars' approaches to learning that can also be labelled experientially-based but not experientially-limited (Lather, 1991; Belenky et al., 1986).

This rejection of the simple transference of workplace learning to the academy should not be read as a rejection of the idea that some work-based learning is not useful, or indeed credit worthy. Nor should it be taken as an argument that working people are not capable of breaking through the workplace ideology designed to co-opt their compliance. (For an interesting illumination and discussion of both these points and a detailed examination of the complexities of learning practices see Sawchuk's *Adult Learning and Technology in Working-Class Life*, 2003.) What the above discussion is arguing is that any claim for extensive transference of workplace learning into higher education credits needs to be critically examined; the silences and absences—what has not been learned—may be as important as the knowledge claimed.

Nor is this an argument suggesting the academy has a stranglehold on what counts as knowledge. For example, women's studies, labour studies, indigenous knowledge, cultural studies (Steele, 1997), and the study of adult education all began life outside of the main halls and cloisters of the established universities. And mainstream education today still downplays or ignores the experience of minority groups in society such that their own learning about whom they are and what place they occupy within the dominant culture is undertaken outside the official curriculum (Kelly, 1998; 2004). This illustrates that knowledge originating and gained outside of universities is important and critical experiential learning or nonformal education is relevant to some programs. (A further question that cannot be explored here but should be acknowledged is how do we change those conservative university programs that don't pose critical questions?)

In relation to the argument for PLAR as a mechanism for increasing access it should be noted that the evidence to date does not support a view that PLAR generally has increased access for educationally marginal and disadvantaged groups. A comparative study of European provision found that PLAR did not particularly advantage the disadvantaged but like many other educational schemes was utilized more by those who already enjoyed some privilege

(European Commission, 2002). Perhaps this is an argument for targeted PLAR schemes aimed at particular social or occupational categories such as labour studies or nursing discussed below. PLAR has been advocated in South Africa as a counter-balance to educational disadvantage resulting from years of apartheid and is claimed to be increasing access there (Cooper and Walters, 2009; Peters, 2001; Andersson and Harris, 2006).

Workplace Learning and PLAR

As illustrated in the introduction to this section, much of the energy behind the recognition for prior learning is coming from the workplace. The argument for PLAR of vocational skills comes in many forms and from many different directions. In some cases unions are arguing that their members are undervalued, that their skills and knowledge are not being recognized or rewarded; in other circumstances, employers are pushing PLAR, arguing that with PLAR in place training and credentializing can be speeded up and unnecessary duplication avoided. From another perspective, individual employees may want PLAR to enhance their promotion possibilities. PLAR of vocational skills may seem obvious and relatively straightforward but there are still issues that need to be addressed. These include some of the "tolerable contradictions" referred to by Alan Thomas (1998) - who will decide what counts and what does not, and will college enrolments fall or will PLAR boost student numbers? Some of the issues become many-sided; for example, what level of competence equals what skill, what is the relationship between apprenticeship and PLAR? (Individual workers, different unions, and different employers may line up differently on such questions.)

Beyond the above concerns, it may be possible to institute forms of PLAR that do grant advanced standing/course credits to mature students through the recognition that their prior learning is extensive and deserving of credit. The rationale for doing this is simple enough; most certificate and degree courses are designed to ground students in an area of knowledge and assume no prior knowledge beyond what could be expected from a high school student. Even when targeted at more mature students, they are mimicked on programs of study designed for graduating high school students. Adult students may not need to undergo the exact same journey to arrive at the overall understanding of a particular subject area.

For example, a student who has held a number of positions in her or his union over a number of years is likely to have insights and understandings that go beyond those that can be expected from the average eighteen-year-old or from another adult student with no such experience. If she or he is enrolled in a labour studies program, it is likely that the student with a rich life experience can, as outlined above, demonstrate credit-worthy knowledge relevant to the program.

A similar argument can be made for students engaged in other areas of study with prior program related areas of knowledge (social work, nursing, business, etc). In the case of the labour studies student, it may also be possible to grant some credit for non-credit union education courses undertaken as well as for the experiential knowledge gained through union activity. Nurses taking internal training courses and gaining knowledge through experience on the job woud be another example. This may result in a student doing fewer university courses, but they will still have to take some. It does not exclude the student from undertaking the hard grind of course work or from the tasks of critical reading and writing that is associated with academic work. What it does do is accept that learning outside of the academy is valuable and relevant; it may be different learning from course-based learning but it can, nonetheless, result in valuable knowledge, some of which will be "credit-worthy."[1]

PLAR at Work

Given the impetus for granting PLAR in higher education came from business interests it may appear to be surprising how little use is made of it within workplaces when considering workers skill levels needed for upgrading and promotions. Employers may use "skills profiling" from time to time or simply observational methods for determining workers' readiness for upgrading or promotions (in-house, for management eyes only) Perhaps one of the reasons they do not want a more formal public PLAR process stems from fears that something like the Australian experience will appear. In Australia the opportunity existed for workers to demonstrate knowledge that could reach up to the next skill category on the nationally agreed occupational/skills ladder and then of course the question became will the employer pay the agreed rate "for knowledge" in

1 For a more complete discussion of the issues raised above, see Spencer & Kelly, 2005.

that category rather than just the going rate for the job currently being performed?

Summary on PLAR

In summary it can be argued that credit can be granted on a modular or course-by-course basis or as program credits. Building PLAR into programs can have a significant impact resulting in a program tailored to meet mature student needs (Peters, 2001). However, any claim for extensive transference of experiential learning into higher education credits needs to be critically examined if it is to gain the support of academics. As Hanson has commented "rigorous though the technical requirements of PLA may be they are of little help without a clear understanding of what they are measuring against and why" (1997. p. 11).

Accelerating an adult student to achieve degree completion may result in them missing out on crucial areas of knowledge and critical insights and understandings. In the end the DaimlerChrysler employees refereed to at the start of this chapter may have got their degree but were they denied an education? On the other hand adult students do not have to travel the same road to a degree as a high school leaver; for example, adult life experiences may legitimately replace elective courses designed to give "breadth" for younger students, even if it cannot substitute for core courses.

One of the challenges for PLAR advocates and reluctant academics alike is to overcome the "with us or against us" attitude that pervades debate about PLAR and engage in critical evaluation of the value and applicability of PLAR in particular programs. While PLAR may emphasize access (dramatically illustrated in post-apartheid South Africa but little evidenced in Europe) and has the potential to shake up traditional teaching, the mainstream promotion of PLAR does little to resuscitate the democratic social purposes of adult education. It has the opposite tendency; it emphasizes the argument that learning is essentially about skills and competencies useful for employment.

The challenge for progressive educators is to marry the critical experiential learning that working people do engage in to critical theoretical knowledge within the academy: to recognize experiential knowledge when it is appropriate and build on it when needed. Under the right circumstances workplace learning, along with other experiential and non-credit learning, can contribute to higher education and can do so by enhancing rather than diminishing the case for a radical higher education: that is for an academy that becomes a "critical agency, facilitating the symbiosis between academic, theoretical knowledge and practical, lived experience in the 'real world'" (Taylor et al., 2002, p. 135).

Work and Learning in the Academy

Before moving away from post-secondary education we should have a quick look at work and learning within the academy itself—the academy as a work-site. Our focus here will be on university staff accepting a role for the university as an institution supporting neo-liberal values and corporate agendas, and accepting hierarchical administrative structures replacing a quasi-democratic tradition of collegial governance developed from the traditional notion of the university as an "academy of self-governing scholars." Although some writers would question an assertion that the academy generally has capitulated to the neo-liberal agenda and has accepted corporatization of university affairs, we would argue the above generalization is true for a majority of the academy and that these agendas and perspectives are increasingly mirrored within university culture, especially in the undermining of collegial governance within the academy, in faculty reward systems including annual assessments of "outputs," and in student evaluations of faculty.

As argued elsewhere the members of the university community are engaged in forms of learning that are neither neutral nor innocent. The problematic result of such learning is that many students, instructors, and others involved come to see the university as a purveyor of a valued commodity and, consequently, produce for themselves identities ("neo-liberal selves," Davies & Petersen, 2005) congruous with these neo-liberal ideologies.[2]

A critical understanding of meaning-making and adult learning within the academy might also help theorists of higher and adult education, management or organizational studies, and all those studying work and learning understand how the production of meaning at other work-sites is not a neutral process but is, as argued in this text, influenced by culture and ideology. Many academics working

---

2 See Kelly & Yochim, 2011, for a fuller discussion in relation to university student ratings of professors.

in higher education are engaged in forms of learning which are "political" rather than "neutral" and which can dovetail seamlessly with neo-liberal ideology if accepted by university staff un-reflexively and without challenge. This is particularly true for university administrators whose concern is to create evaluation of educational tools without regard to the cultural or political consequences.

Those investigating how academics have become seduced by neo-liberal university practices have noted how the process has unfolded, with parts of the puzzle to be found in general cuts in public funding, and in shifts towards more "practical" or professional degree programs and "applied universities," and in tying research increasingly to private funders. In addition, assessment and promotion are increasingly tied to measurable outputs, which in many cases produces more and more research that is of less value than before. Bronwyn Davies writing for the Australian Academy of Social Sciences explains it in these terms:

> In the ambivalent take-up of neo-liberal discourses and practices some of the academics I interviewed work incredibly hard to forge a pathway that is successful in neo-liberal terms. Some find in the encouragement to entrepreneurial activity some opportunities coming up that they would not have had otherwise. All work harder than they have ever worked before, but none claimed to be producing better work than they had done before. Many said, like the interviewee above, that sustaining quality work was not possible in the new system. Some were angry and grieved at their inability to do sustained intellectual work as they finished off the reports for one research grant and then dived into the production of the next. Many describe serious health problems that require a disciplined regimen of working on their bodies to keep them fit enough and healthy enough to survive. Even with an ambivalent and partial take-up of neo-liberal discourses and practices, hearts and hands follow the head in the production of endless doing that saps the body of energy, deadens the spirit and troubles the heart. (2005, p. 36)

Aspects of the "new managerialism"—a term once favoured in Australia in place of neo-liberalism (Davies, 2003)—as applied to measuring student/faculty interaction is particularly problematic when considering mature students or the teaching of adult education students given that adult education scholars value student experience and insight as a key component of their teaching. Understood in this way it can be seen that, for example, the connection between faculty evaluation of students (in a highly competitive neo-liberal university) and subsequent student evaluation of faculty does not promote a truly dialogic adult learning environment (à la Freire, 1970). For example, many students of adult education have to be challenged to question deeply-held convictions, beliefs, and values if they are going to be adult educators in the "social purpose" tradition of adult education (Collins, 1991; Welton, 2005; Spencer & Lange, 2013). Evaluation processes can work against this outcome with "uncomfortable," challenged students rating the professor poorly at the end of the class even if they come to appreciate the benefits twelve months later.

The contemporary university has undergone radical transformation in these neo-liberal times (as argued by Davies & Petersen, 2005; Olssen & Peters, 2005; Jones, 2004; Taylor, Barr, & Steele, 2002 and others). Many of these writers call for a re-stating of traditional liberal university values including critical understandings of society. However as Gary Hall (2004) argues (in relation to cultural studies but it applies across disciplines):

> [the] necessity of thinking about the university ... is something that has frequently been overlooked within cultural studies. ... All too often such "theoretical" self-reflection is regarded as taking away from the real business of cultural studies ... concerned with practical, material, political and economic issues in the world beyond the institution. (p. 1)

In other words, many potentially radical academics have not critically examined their own workplaces as sites of power to the same degree that they may have looked at other workplaces they investigate. The reasons for this failure are without question numerous and complex. Yet given the historical connection of interdisciplinary studies to adult education (see Steele, 1997, for the link to cultural studies), and the often contentious relationship between the state and the institutionalized form of some academic studies, it is nonetheless puzzling.

As argued previously neo-liberal values permeate the governance and management of education becoming normalized and absorbed by staff including faculty and result in reproduction: to repeat Mitchell's (2003) comment from the previous chapter:

> those pushing a neo-liberal agenda in education stress ... the necessity for greater ... accountability and the imperative to create hierarchically conditioned, globally oriented state subjects (p. 388).

In considering what universities are, Collini (2012) has commented: "once upon a time it was the role of governments to provide for the needs of universities; but now universities are deemed to provide for the needs of governments," which can be read as to serve the "needs" of the global economy.

The Corporate University

Although the move towards corporate neo-liberal universities has accelerated in recent times—particularly with corporations setting up their own "universities" and for-profit universities such as Phoenix becoming established—the shift to the "corporate" university has a long history. In 1970 E.P. Thompson and colleagues documented student protests to this shift in *Warwick University Ltd.*

Thompson argued that many academics were quick to side with the university administration and were more concerned with their own careers than with academic freedom. He observed the "enormous pomp and propriety of the self-important academic" a species he described as *Academicus Superciliosus*. He continued:

> The behaviour patterns of one of the true members of the species are unmistakable. He is inflated with self-esteem and perpetually self-congratulatory as to the high vocation of the university teacher; but he knows almost nothing about any other vocation, and he will lie down and let himself be walked over if anyone enters from the outer world who has money or power or even a tough line on realist talk ...
>
> Academic freedom is forever on their lips, and is forever disregarded in their actions. They are the last people to whom it can be safely entrusted, since the present moment is never the opportune moment to stand and fight.

He also makes reference to "crafty calculations of short-term advantages" including "that chance of promotion" and an ability to "scurry furiously and self-importantly around in committees like a white mouse running in a wheel, while his master is carrying him, cage and all, to be sold at the local pet-shop."

A bit harsh maybe, and written in the context of student protests, but it still rings true, particularly in relation to some academics' support for hierarchical reward systems with varied annual incremental awards essentially based on individualistic goals—a sure-fire way to seduce some academics to support the neo-liberal, corporate university.

CHAPTER 7

Transitions, Gender, and Difference: Training and Skills

In this chapter we will introduce a matrix of workplace learning issues ranging from the position of women and cultural difference at work, to approaches to training and skills. We begin with the idea that work and learning can be viewed from the lens of "transitions" in learning including considering the role and value of volunteering as job preparation and transitions as a way of viewing technology and training. In two distinct sections we discuss gender and difference at work, and skills and training, while retaining the concept of transitions, as well as explaining competency-based training. We finish the chapter with a note on training and program planning as distinctive areas of study.

Transitions

A text edited by Peter Sawchuk and Alison Taylor (2010) provides an insightful introductory chapter that demonstrates a way for readers to understand the work and learning literature and make sense of the field. It's not the only way to consider work and learning scholarship but their approach has a coherence that allows for explorations that go beyond the simplistic school-to-work emphasis, or supply-side economic solutions of training/education for jobs, or investing in human capital to fit into the "knowledge economy" (a phrase beloved by political commentators but as we have seen so absent from the lives of most Canadian workers).

Sawchuk and Taylor approach learning and work transitions as "increasingly complex, extended across the life course, differentiated and in turn differentiating across social groups" and they also adopt what they call an "expanded critical vocationalism approach to learning/work transitions" that recognizes context, difference, and power as well as informal practices/learning (2010, p. 1). This can be contrasted with new vocationalism, which emphasizes a move away from specific skills and knowledge training into flexibility, teamwork, adaptability, etc.—all allied to the needs of a supposed "knowledge economy" emphasizing the importance of workers investing in their own human capital in order to qualify for multiple job opportunities in the claimed "post-industrial," "post-capitalist" economy and labour market.

There are a range of perspectives adopted by writers in the field, some favouring aspects of new vocationalism while others more aware of critical vocationalism. Sawchuk and Taylor's edited book was intended to be located at the critical vocationalism end of the spectrum and most contributors succeed in indentifying key markers of the critical paradigm. although as with most edited texts there is some unevenness. However, the contributions can be read as providing case study evidence supporting the core ideas about the importance of difference/identity and unequal power as well as informal learning.

In addition to the editors' introduction and afterword there are chapters covering such topics as youth, immigration/racialization, women in trades, volunteer work, ability/disability, a bio-pharmaceutical case study, retirement, and an interesting examination of the social relations and labour process in a college program. Some of this material may be familiar but is nonetheless valuable while others are introducing new research, insights, and understandings of work and learning scholarship centred on the notion of learning/work transitions. Therefore the idea of transitions particularly from a critical vocational perspective provides a useful framework for examining how gender intersects with other issues and for understanding training and skills.

An example, which at first sight does not appear central to our concerns, is by Slade and Schugurensky, focussed on volunteerism. The authors write about employers requiring "Canadian work experience" of new immigrants as a "catch 22." Given that few employers will employ them, how does an immigrant professional get a year's employment experience? Volunteering was seen as one way to gain Canadian experience and agencies encouraged this view. But Slade and Schugurensky's study revealed that immigrants recognized that employers did not value volunteering and the data in the study supported this view—87% of participants in the study: "were either unemployed or underemployed even after getting their Canadian work experience through volunteering" (2010, p. 277).

The study also reported that many volunteers did unpaid work alongside paid employees and the study participants wanted research to "examine the conditions under which highly skilled racialized immigrants are working for free" (p. 278). The authors also noted that much of this volunteerism was in "for-profit companies." In addition many volunteers did not feel they "freely chose to volunteer"; it could be regarded as "coerced volunteerism" (p. 278).

Transitions: Technology and Training

Another chapter in the *Challenging Transitions in Learning and Work* text, this one by Sawchuk, which takes us back to an earlier study (Hennessy & Sawchuk, 2003) reported on in Chapter 3, but this time more focussed on learning and training at the work-site. As noted, the workers were being moved from a people-oriented service with social work elements, one in which independent critical thinking, conflict resolution, and team work skills were being replaced by a "vision of welfare work defined by 'moving through screens' and administering funds" (2010, p. 204). The work was "being shifted from professional, or semi-professional to clerical" (p. 192).

The survey conducted to find out who was having difficulties with the new technology training (veteran worker or younger newbie) did not reveal that older workers had significantly lower comfort level with technology or computer competency but did reveal that there was a frustration experienced by veteran workers with the inflexibility of the technological systems. The workers with the accumulated knowledge (or human capital) were being replaced by those with no historical memory but with top computer skills. On the face of it the workforce appeared to have joined the "post-modern," efficient "knowledge economy" with the extensive use of new technology but in reality it was the reverse; technical knowhow had replaced useful knowledge and accumulated skills (pp. 204-05). Sawchuk is cautious about drawing too many conclusions from this "transition" in work as illustrated in one case study but as noted earlier in Chapter 3 (by Bratton and Brown in particular) we know that technology and work processes work together to determine what level of control workers may have over the labour process, what scope there is for skill and knowledge development, for independent action, and what level of supervision operates. De-skilling and increased supervision can go hand in hand with the introduction of new technology.

Gender and Difference at Work

This discussion of gender and difference at work is intended only as an introduction to a wide ranging topic. The first part looks at "women" and the second more at "culture and difference."

Many discussions of women's learning at work have focussed on top-end jobs and issues such as "the glass ceiling" that effectively prevent women gaining fair representation within higher managerial and professional ranks (and recently also "the glass border" that works against women seeking high managerial posts in international/transnational companies). There has also been a focus on those jobs that are considered "women's work" (such as nursing and elementary teaching) and in many cases limit women in terms of pay and professional status. And finally there is the ever-growing literature on contingent/precarious work which features low-paid racialized women workers, many of whom are recent immigrants to Canada.

It has been generally recognized that appropriate qualifications are more important for women to advance through an organization than they are for men. (For example, the surveys undertaken of Athabasca University students have consistently shown that female more than male students report that their educational qualifications have been key to them gaining promotion or better jobs: more of the male students have progressed without having to refer to their educational qualifications. Note the majority of AU program students are mature, in work, and study part-time.) In general it has been shown that women, and other equity groups, have to "prove" that their abilities and qualifications are relevant for specific jobs, particularly the traditionally male-dominated positions, much more so than is the case for their "white" male, able-bodied counterparts.

Issues of appearance and dress continue to be factors for many female workers, particularly those in the service sector. And, as the spike in claims of sexual harassment in the RCMP in 2012 illustrate, women still have to deal with overt sexism at work and on training programs, again much more than do men.

Analysis of the white-collar or service sector workplace usually discovers women clustered in low-paid clerical support or frontline customer service jobs with few learning opportunities provided to allow these women to move into the next layer of administrative or managerial positions. It is not that women are not represented in the next layer of work hierarchies, it's just that once started in a particular (usually gendered) occupation, such as clerical support, it becomes difficult to progress as the position generally gives little access to progressive training programs. Any training that is available is usually limited to training in their existing job. The women in the middle range administrative positions were usually recruited into the organization at that level and not promoted from the "ghettoized" employment positions of clerical support and front-line service.

None of the above is to suggest that women do not learn at work; like all other workers they learn lots of different things, some job-related, some not. Among other knowledge gained is that of how to survive male-dominated workplaces!

Probert (1999) provides a good overview of the position of women in the workforce and the implications for workplace learning. Interestingly she considers the new work organization as being no more favourable to women than the more traditional forms of gendered work. Critoph (2003) looks in detail at the impact of the transfer of training to the Canadian provinces and thereby provides a unique lens for examining women's work and training opportunities in Canada. She did not find much evidence of progressive training opportunities that addressed systemic inequalities.[1]

It is worth repeating that many women find themselves in low-paid, part-time and casual employment categories and all the studies of women conclude that the work and learning rhetoric and public policy promotion of learning does not benefit them. If anything, it locks them into marginality and cements the exploited nature of their employment. Work and learning (to the extent that vocational learning takes place at all for many of these workers) rarely results in "liberation" or "empowerment" but in the reverse. The learning transition, as identified in Chapter 3, is to "construct themselves as precarious workers" (Mirchandani & Slade, 2002; Mirchandani et al., 2010).

---

[1] Critoph is the opening chapter in Cohen's, 2003, edited collection *Training the Excluded for Work: Access and Equity for Women, Immigrants, First Nations, Youth, and People with Low Incomes,* which provides a number of interesting case studies related to these different social groups, who are often excluded from the world of paid work and particularly from the better-paid male-dominated occupations.

Culture and Difference

As noted in Chapters 2 and 3, organizational behaviour and organizational theory have become popular areas of study on management courses. Much has been made of the importance of organizational culture in the new workplace. Some workplaces are now described as having open, participatory, even democratic work cultures where different ideas are encouraged among a free, creative exchange of views. Again, a cautionary note needs to be signalled at the outset: most organizations remain hierarchical (there really are people at the top making the key decisions). From a workers' perspective they cannot be described as democratic; the bosses were not elected by the workers. These organizations do like all their employees to "share the vision" of the organization and to begin management training by making sure everyone is "on the right page" (comments made by a management trainer at a plenary session of a conference entitled "How to keep your intellectual capital," Calgary, May 1999—with "your" in this case referring to the company's interests). For example, if you work for a large drug company it is unlikely you will have any influence (or a job for very long!) if you happen to believe the patent laws are exploiting the sick or that as a society we have become too dependent on drugs to cure all illness.

Solomon teases out some of the problems associated with trying to celebrate difference when working in a workplace with a "common workplace culture" with "shared belief systems, values and attitudes" (1999, p. 127; see also Solomon, 2001). Her concerns resonate with our discussion of corporate culture in Chapter 2 and our discussion on schooling in Chapter 5. We also need to reflect on the position of contingent workers, particularly those from marginalized social groups, first discussed in Chapter 3.

While there has been a shift in Canada to recognizing ethnic origins as an asset that companies can utilize to their advantage, the basic problem of racialized understandings persist in work and society. From a teacher/trainer perspective, it may appear noble to argue that "all trainees should be treated the same" and in a "colour-blind" fashion, in most cases that only imposes a Eurocentric perspective that denies the historical significance of difference. As Solomon is arguing, trainers need to problematize the issues before they begin their training programs.[2] (See also, Sensoy & DiAngelo, 2012.)

---

[2] There are a number of academic journal articles and books examining these issues of

Skills and Training

Two issues have dominated recent discussion on training and skills. The first is whether workers in Canada (and elsewhere) have sufficient training to equip them for the new world of work.

Generally, government policy in the developed world has (since the mid-1970s) emphasized training, training, and more training as a solution to unemployment, underemployment, and a perceived jobs-training gap. The argument being that if workers have the right training the jobs will follow. During the same period, however, there has been an abandonment of "industry policy" or employment creation policies. (The financial crisis of 2008 sparked a recession and an attempt at stimulating the economy via monetary supply-side policies and, with the exceptions of a few interventionist measures such as the auto-industry rescue plan, these were not direct job retention or job-creation strategies.) In addition, worker's rights to unemployment insurance have been curtailed and linked to recipients being in "re-training" programs, but without any clear vision as to re-training for what jobs. This stance reflects the adoption of neoliberal economic policies that emphasize a reduced role for the state allied to increased freedom for market forces in a global economy. It is what has come to be described as "supply-side economics"—in this instance, a focus on the supply of labour that ignores overall demand for goods and services, and hence more jobs, and the possibilities for direct interventions in the economy. The government policies are not directly focused on "job creation" and increased employment (and certainly not on "good jobs"—full-time, well-paid, etc.) as a target of economic policy.

The second issue is closely related to the first. It is whether workers' existing skills are sufficiently recognized and used in the modern economy. Survey evidence suggests that workers do have extensive knowledge, skills, and even formal credentials that are currently undervalued and underused (Livingstone, 1999a; Wotherspoon, 2009). Constant training and retraining, on this analysis, is a misplaced government policy that has more to do with disciplining the unemployed (no welfare provided unless the recipient is in work

---

gender and difference at work, as well as some popular management magazines and books. As with all HRM and work and learning literature, but perhaps even more so in this case, readers need to choose supplementary readings carefully and read critically in order to expand their understanding of gender, difference, and identity at work.

or in training), cutting public expenditure, and shifting the blame to workers for the lack of job opportunities (Swift, 1995; Cruikshank, 2006).

With the ebb and flow of economic activity, specific skill shortages do occur but there has been little discussion about employers' responsibility for maintaining a consistent supply of trained individuals. The idea that a large employer may maintain an apprenticeship school larger than that just required to meet their own needs (partly as a contribution to the local community and industry) has been supplanted by a management style always focussed on the immediate bottom line–a short term, narrow accounting perspective (Spencer, 1989 p. 43-47)–that does not prevent them from running to different layers of government for assistance when the skill-shortages do emerge. A related change has resulted from the undermining of union influence over apprenticeships–union rules that might have established that for example, for every two journeyman hired there must also be an apprentice, in labour contracts. Contracts that would provide for future skilled workers in a particular trade have therefore been undermined by aggressive management bargaining and by the general weakening of union influence and union density within the overall working population.

An interesting study by Statistics Canada, *The Dynamics of Overqualification: Canada's Unemployed University Graduates* (described in Li, Gervais & Duval, 2006), surveyed 30,000 adults from 1991–2001 and found that one in five university graduates worked in jobs that required a high school diploma or less; that younger workers, immigrants, and commerce graduates were more likely to be overqualified and were found in the retail and wholesale sector. They also concluded that overqualification had an important impact in terms of frustration with lower wages and job dissatisfaction and concluded this situation represented an underutilization of human capital.

It must be recognized that some of these workers may have chosen not to work in a more professional category and that having a university degree (or two) does not guarantee anyone a job, but nonetheless the study does tend to support the argument that in Canada workers are generally more qualified and skilled than the available jobs. The gap is not so much of workers not having the skills but more of the paucity of available skilled/knowledge work. The focus of the media is on the "failure" of the post-secondary system to provide education and training to meet corporate needs and yet many graduates report that they have few regrets about their educational experience (outside of the costs incurred). The disappointment they experience is with the inability of employers to provide engaging employment opportunities whether or not the employment is in a preferred area or related to their education. Generally the media, given its desire to represent the supply-side neo-liberal argument, consistently overlooks the implications of this opinion.

Education for Economy

It's worth re-stating that the emphasis by Human Resources and Skills Development Canada has been to co-opt adult education into a training focus; an example is the study *Determinants of Formal and Informal Canadian Adult Learning: Insights from the Adult Education and Training Surveys* (2007). The abstract makes it clear:

> The urgency of expanding adult learning to support economic growth and higher living standards has put the focus on adults' readiness to engage in learning. In a time of evidence-based policy making there is a growing need to develop a better understanding of the factors that determine participation in adult education and training. (p. 1)

Evidence-based policy always sounds so grand and definitive but in reality it rarely is; there is always competing "evidence" and interpretations of evidence that require selections to be made along with predictions as to future employment opportunities (Clegg, 2005). However, other issues flow from these concerns. Should learning (particularly vocational training) be competency-based or holistic, and what kinds of learning are relevant in the workplace–formal or non-formal courses, or just informal learning–and should we focus on learning theories that are relevant to the workplace, such as "feedback," "feedforward," and "doubleloop"?[3] There are also issues raised by the demand for the recognition of prior learning, particularly workplace learning, in training schemes and in the formal education system as discussed in Chapter 6. The workplace is also a site of literacy and basic education for adults and second/additional-language learning. The multi-dimensional nature of these issues

[3] Learning theory has entered into the workplace learning discourse, but it is unclear what its contribution is, given its often blatant disregard for the issues of power and control that permeate workplace relations.

means that a simple demand for "reform" of the post-secondary system is unlikely to have desired results.

The abstract above also begs the question as to whether "higher economic growth" can be achieved without long-term and irreversible environmental costs—so far, EJ Misham's 1967 warnings about *The Costs of Economic Growth* are going unheeded even as every year that passes they appear to be more germane—and if not, adult learning should not be "supporting" such a goal. Also do we need "higher living standards" for all as suggested by HRSDC or do we want a more equitable distribution of existing wealth and power—perhaps within the context of a sustainable and "ethical economy" with an expanded community-owned "commons" rather than individual ownership of value as described by Adam Arvidsson and Nicolai Peitersen (2013), Slavoj Zizek (2012), and others? The more we think about the HRSDC position the more we have to conclude that it is exactly what we don't want adult learning to be about. The "urgency" for an expanded work and learning scholarship is perhaps to help adults cope with transitions that are "increasingly complex (and) extended across the life course."

Other questions include who gets training? Most reports indicate the more educated a worker and the higher they are in the workplace hierarchy the more employer-paid training is available: manual workers in lower-pay grades get least—limited perhaps to basic, and often biased, safety training plus some "basic skills" or literacy training. If you are a temporary worker even less training is available; and "marginal" workers may have some access to some basic education but little else (Goldberg, 2006; Jackson, 2005: also see Fenwick, 2006b, for a critique of the Canadian essential skills/ work skills initiatives as too fixated on a prescribed, somewhat rigid, interpretation of essential work skills).

There have been some studies of more imaginative and collaborative training schemes and programs. An early collection edited by Maurice Taylor, *Workplace Education: The Changing Landscape*, was published in 1997 and represented much of the change taking place in the work and learning/training practices in Canada in the mid-1990s (the text also included some international experience). A number of the twenty-three chapters adopted a critical analytical take on the case studies and examples discussed in the collection; they ranged across issues of workplace learning, partnerships and government, sectors council, and corporate training programs. Other reports of case studies or particular provincial and/or sector training programs or on work and learning generally have been produced since but none of the later collections matched Taylor's sampling of the then current Canadian workplace learning issues and examples. One of the problems experienced since this 1997 publication has been the decline in industry sector councils that included union representation and the general withdrawal of governments for their support of tripartite (government, industry, and union) meetings and discussions of issues. There has also been a switch in policy favouring independent corporate and industry procedures and actions, excluding union and/or worker representation—the marketplace replacing a more pluralist vision of society.

Another problem referred to in the introduction to our text is the multidisciplinary nature of the field of study of learning and work. To review what studies have taken place in relation to skills training would require an identification of what skills we should investigate. As Peter Sawchuk (2011) has noted the field has become complex:

> The multi-disciplinarity of the literature has seen a proliferation of identified skill types: from common notions of "soft" and "hard" skills, general education and vocationally specific skills, literacy, communication, comprehension, multi-tasking skills, procedural and declarative knowledge, through to somewhat more theoretically robust formulations of such things as work-related emotional skill, articulation skill, relational skills and aesthetic skill. And, the proliferation (helpful, rhetorical or otherwise) does not end there (p. 141).

The discussions of "transitions, gender and difference, training and skills" in this chapter are intended to be indicative of some of the perspectives and problems that could be highlighted in, and associated with, the mainstream work and learning literature. Readers will of course have their own experiences of these issues that need to be reflected on alongside the more eclectic arguments presented here.[4]

---

[4] The study of training and skills development has spurned a different literature, much of it instrumental in orientation, and care needs to be taken in searching out material that acknowledges the context of neo-liberal ideology, power relations, and cultural awareness. "Program planning" is another sub-set of adult education that has developed along more critical lines in recent years in response to earlier work by Cervero and Wilson, whose recent text is entitled *Working the Planning Table: Negotiating Democratically for Adult, Continuing and Workplace Education* (2006). In recognition of these distinctive literatures, universities often offer courses in these areas, for example Athabasca University offers graduate and undergraduate courses on "the Canadian training system," "program planning," and "work and learning."

Competency-Based Training

Training and educational objectives are increasingly being expressed as "learning outcomes" that is in terms of specific "competencies" to be achieved. Particular skills are broken down into a series of incremental steps or competencies and, in theory, trainees can only move on to the next competency when the present one has been mastered. Each level of training fits into the next one as long as the competencies have been achieved. There are a number of problems with this behaviourist approach common in North America–four of which are:

- Compartmentalization and fragmentation of knowledge occurs (Collins, 1991)
- There are practical limitations of breaking down all skills into detailed sub-sets of skill prerequisites
- Not every student will learn along a specific path or require mastery at one step prior to gaining competency at the next
- This approach ignores a more holistic approach to "competency" that was popular in Europe–an approach inclusive of life-skills, participatory and community skills (English & Mayo, 2012, p. 97–98).

In spite of these limitations, competency-based programs are being extended beyond mechanical or motor skills to include communication, collective (team work), and representational (team leadership, representing fellow workers) skills and other "soft" skills. Although these kinds of changes, together with a looser definition of competencies and relaxing the necessity of prerequisites for any particular skill or educational achievement, may save this concept from impracticality it remains a limited educational approach. It favours a narrow mechanistic training over education and the acquisition of particular skills over a more holistic and critical adult education (see Peruniak, 1997, for a fuller discussion).

CHAPTER 8

The Challenge of Democratizing Work and Learning in a Global Economy

In this chapter we are centrally concerned with the challenges of democratizing work and learning, empowering workers, and responding to the problems of globalization. We open with an example of work in the globalized economy, what it means to shift production to the "economic south" and specifically the Spectrum Sweater factory collapse. We attempt to draw some conclusions from that tragedy. The next section begins with a discussion on the democratization of work with a few observations before reviewing the ideas behind participatory strategic HRM. This is followed by examining an example of empowerment at work—the Mondragon co-operatives of northern Spain. We outline the co-operatives' success in meeting its original purpose of creating jobs and examine Mondragon's record on running the co-operatives. The final section reviews the experience of the co-operatives during recession and growth before progressing to a brief discussion on other co-operatives and of how Mondragon is being considered as an example of worker-centred economic development and worker empowerment in North America and serves as a positive conclusion to this text.

Globalization and the "Economic South"

The movement of production to less economically developed countries by some transnational corporations does provide a challenge to international agencies and unions concerned with establishing decent work and conditions, including meaningful workplace learning. This production tends to be located in countries with low labour costs, no tradition of independent unionization, few minimum labour laws, or health and safety standards (and no effective inspection/regulation), and "economic" or "free trade" zones which may be isolated from towns and are set up to attract foreign investment with the promise of a cheap, compliant workforce. In many cases these are assembly plants utilizing young female employees who have to live in the zone area, who may be subject to physical and sexual abuse. The opportunities for "learning" let alone "empowerment" are severely constrained.

To combat these conditions, international agencies, international union federations, and some individual unions (sometimes working with NGOs) have pursued parent company compliance with "codes of practice," "social auditing," or other mechanisms by which companies agree to monitor working conditions in their suppliers. More recently international union federations have reached "framework agreements" with corporation head offices which push them to only do business with suppliers who recognize workers' rights and independent unions. As we write, the UN *Protect, Respect, Remedy: Framework for Business and Human Rights* is being developed. It is difficult to predict whether or not these measures will be successful in accelerating working conditions in countries such as Bangladesh, Indonesia, the Philippines, Thailand, and China. We cannot celebrate a new approach to "work and learning," "learning organizations," or "quality work" in the "economic north" if the food we eat, the shoes on our feet, the clothes on our back, and the computer at our fingertips are produced under sweat-shop conditions in the "economic south." These conditions include not just unsafe work and unsafe buildings, but the use of child labour and reports of workers committing suicide in response to their inhumane treatment. We begin with an example of what can happen as a result of globalized production.

The Spectrum Sweater Factory Collapse

On April 11, 2005, a factory in Savar, Bangladesh (near Dhaka), making sweaters and T-shirts for the European market collapsed during the nightshift resulting in the deaths of sity-two workers and injury to another eighty-four. Doug Miller[1] has documented this tragedy and the attempts by unions, NGOs, and some buyers to improve the derisory compensation scheme in operation and provide relief for the families and displaced workers at the factory (2012).

As the author notes, this was at the time probably the worst disaster in the clothing industry since the Triangle Shirtwaist Fire in New York in 1911 and it resulted in a sustained international campaign to make multinationals accountable for labour rights abuses which,

---

[1] Emeritus Professor of Worker Rights in Fashion, Northumbria University at Newcastle, United Kingdom.

because of the woeful state of health and safety in the Ready Made Garments Industry (RMG), continue to this day. Miller presents a detailed inside account of that campaign and to our knowledge is the first in-depth case study which addresses the problems and complexities of resolving international disputes in outsourced supply chains, and most certainly the first in the apparel sector.

Last Nightshift in Savar

The book places the disaster in its wider context opening with a brief history of sweated labour and of the origins of "sweating" and the RMG industry in Bangladesh. Chapter 2 describes the factory collapse and the third chapter grapples with the issue of cause and culpability; Chapter 4 looks at the response and mobilization of groups in Bangladesh and Chapter 5 at the international solidarity campaign and the reaction of the buyers. While the international (and local) unions did not have representation at the plant, they did seek to represent the workers and win compensation and benefits from government, employers, and buyers. The campaign was union and NGO led (most notably the International Textile, Garment and Leather Workers Federation, ITGLWF, and the Clean Clothes Campaign, CCC) and their pressure resulted in the European buyers taking two quite distinct approaches–a rights based pension scheme versus a relief and income generation initiative. Woven into the account are the thoughts and actions of some of the key protagonists–Javier Chercolés, the director of Corporate Social Responsibility at Inditex, and, in particular, the late Neil Kearney, General Secretary of ITGLWF, who made this a personal commitment to win adequate compensation and to use the disaster as a building block to gain improved health and safety legislation and practices for Bangladesh and other less developed countries.

Chapter 6 is focussed on the operation of the two emerging (rights based and income generation relief schemes). The chapter also explains some of the difficulties encountered in administering a rights based scheme in the context of the cultural norms prevailing in Bangladesh, particularly in relation to the widows of those sweater operators who perished in the disaster. Chapter 7 attempts to assess the outcomes from the collapse and all the actions and schemes which followed and Chapter 8 discusses the limits and possibilities of corporate responsibility in outsourced multi buyer operations. *Last Nightshift in Savar* is a multi-dimensional detailed study with both breadth and depth.

There are some important lessons which can be drawn from Doug Miller's narrative, particularly about the ways in which NGOs can work with unions (including international federations) in a society where trade union membership is still viewed as anathema and where union density in the RMG remains low. But the account also tells us about the importance of human agency in adversity in what is an unusual story of how a union general secretary and a head of corporate social responsibility in a major fashion multinational became friends and worked together to improve relief in tragic circumstances.

The account of the *Last Nightshift in Savar* is a major contribution to understanding and hopefully addressing the persistent health and safety malaise which continues to dog the RMG in Bangladesh today. Fresh calls for prevention and improved worker compensation have seen the focus shift to North American brands which have been implicated in a number of recent offshore supplier factory fires, particularly in Pakistan (300 deaths reported in September 2012, in just one fire in Karachi; there have been more fires). For these companies their drive to use cheap labour has now come at its true cost.

At one level these are dramatic and tragic examples of the failure of corporate "work and learning." Its as if nothing was learned from the struggles for factory legislation (in addition to safety and fire regulations, the factory acts also excluded child labour and limits on the hours of work) in the nineteenth and early twentieth century that stressed the importance of proper regulation, inspection, and a "safe work environment." The echoes of the screams from the Triangle Shirtwaist Fire in New York in 1911 are heard 100 years later in Savar and Karachi. It is clearly not enough for companies to adopt new participatory structures at home while ignoring (or doing little about) production conditions overseas. Companies that choose outsourcing of production (including the very profitable and trendy Apple electronics) are opening themselves up to all the accusations of labour abuses even with company monitoring and they are choosing to do this rather than running and operating their own factories. (Could this be considered another example of "harnessed to the money-code the business organisation is actually learning disabled. It is intensely pressurised to learn along a single trajectory: to enhance shareholder profits and interests?" Welton, 2005, p. 100.)

These examples are another reason to consider advocating for the displacement of transnational corporations, including the corporate exploitation of cheap sweat-shop labour, with worker-owned co-operative ventures both at home and abroad. (In the fall of 2012, Apple announced that it will be assembling a "made-in-America" computer, but it is not known if it will use foreign-made parts or allow unions to represent the workers involved.)

The Democratization of Work

The claims of advocates of learning organizations that the processes involved can lead to employee empowerment and eventually workplace democracy are rarely tested against actual experience or against examples of more purposeful democratic organizations. In looking at democratizing work and learning we need to recognize, as noted in the opening chapter, the importance of different organizations—not just private companies and publicly owned (shareholder-owned) corporations but smaller privately owned family firms, publicly provided services, not-for-profit organizations, NGOs, and worker-owned co-operatives.

We also need to stress the importance of unionization as a key element of "industrial democracy," particularly in larger organizations. Too many writers on work and learning fail to recognize the importance of power relations at work and how unions can provide a countervailing power to that concentration of power wielded by management and owners when discussing workplace learning issues. There should be no place for the kind of open hostility towards unions displayed in the media in the work and learning literature. Of course unions must be subject to critical analysis along with other organizations, but to challenge the right of workers to organize and collectively bargain is to deny a key element of democracy at work, an attitude that can only stem from an elitist belief that the workplace should be beyond democratic goals and under the sole control of owners/management. This reflects a belief that it's legitimate for workers to be treated as "resources" not as citizens—citizens with democratic rights even when at work.

Participatory Strategic HRM

The new developments in work and learning are often claimed to be leading to new participatory work and even a new workplace democracy. The commentary that follows reviews some of these arguments and then introduces you to some of the issues facing an actual worker-owned enterprise: an overview of the Mondragon worker-owned co-operatives is presented, contrasting employee empowerment at Mondragon with the claims for employee empowerment in privately owned corporations.

The recent development of new strategic HRM policies focussed on work and learning, learning organizations, and "participatory" structures into a central plank of company policy as argued throughout this book has heightened the debates about the nature of HRM and workplace democracy. HRM has always been more concerned with maximizing the output from employees than with employee welfare, and recent attempts to involve workers and their unions more in decentralized company decision-making combined with increased employee responsibility are, in most organizations, designed ultimately to maximize company output and profit.

Corporations have experimented with a continual stream of schemes claiming to increase job satisfaction for workers and cut company costs. What drives this phenomenon is the dual realization that in traditional companies employers are not very interested in what workers think, and many employees have little control over how they spend their time at work. Therefore, it is argued, workers feel alienated from their work. If employers want employee loyalty, they must improve the quality of work life (QWL). Another driving force is the perceived need to meet the competitive challenge, to match what was often referred to as "Japanese" management techniques, and generally to cut out "waste." This "need" has led to a range of approaches including just-in-time (JIT) stock control, self-directed work teams, cell production, total quality management (TQM), and other employee involvement schemes including the "re-engineering" of the organization. Some argue that, regardless of the origins of these new methods, current HRM practices lead to better treatment of employees, including the increased potential for workplace learning, than in earlier times (or in traditionally managed organizations). However, while this claim might be true for some workers, particularly those in professional or skilled occupations (the key members of the core workforce), it is not necessarily the case for all employees.

The concerns first expressed in manufacturing companies have spread to service companies and public-sector organizations. Consultants spreading this new gospel abound; this revived version of "human capital theory" emphasizes the competitive edge to be gained from a committed, skilled workforce, one that is learning to tackle company problems in new ways including utilizing their "emotional labour."

As previously argued, some of the writing in this area stems from a belief that we are now living in a post-bureaucratic, post-Fordist, post-industrial, post-modern, even post-capitalist society and that Fordist mass production techniques based on Frederick Taylor's "scientific management" approach to work organization are no longer appropriate. Some authors also see adversarial union attitudes as inappropriate in this perceived "new climate." It is claimed that under "Toyotarist" production methods (teams, company unions, JIT, TQM, *Kaizen,* i.e., continuous improvement) decisions are based locally, in "cells." Hence, Toyotarist production is depicted as collaborative, in contrast with "Fordist" machine-paced assembly lines, which are seen as alienating. Claims are made that production is more differentiated than it used to be, that companies compete more on quality than price, and that, therefore, employees must be "empowered" to produce goods and services of high quality.

However, as argued earlier, although there has been a shift away from mass production techniques in industry, an extension of service employment, and a move towards smaller production units, many of the jobs in both services and industry remain repetitive, largely unchallenging and low paid. For example, employment in fast-food outlets, often referred to as "McJobs," are low-skill and low-paid, part-time jobs—rarely empowering in any meaningful sense. The significance of any shift to a "post-industrial" society and towards new participatory management styles is therefore overstated. This is particularly true if you consider the new HRM participatory practices are often combined with downsizing, outsourcing, and the exploitation of global cheap labour.

Many of the accounts recording the successes to be gained by implementing new HRM techniques are written by management consultants who have a vested interest in its continuance. Supporters of this new management style emphasize greater worker control over the design of jobs, more worker contributions to the functioning of the organization, reduced absenteeism, and major cost savings. Some of the relative merits of these claims are questionable and have been discussed in earlier chapters: there is no guarantee that adoption of these policies will save workers' jobs or save a company from bankruptcy.

As noted in Chapter 2 much of the literature celebrating these new HRM methods describes these policies as creating a "sense of shared ownership" and control of the enterprise, however, is not the same thing as workers actually owning and controlling.

While participatory strategic HRM companies (learning organizations) are often contrasted with traditionally managed companies, they are rarely compared to actual worker-owned enterprises in which worker job-control and empowerment might be considered more complete. While the omission might be understandable for companies and consultants, students of work and learning should contrast these claims and participatory techniques with other, more radical models based on the ideas of workers' ownership and co-operation (and even with more limited worker influenced structures, such as social enterprises and extensive Employee Stock Ownership Plans, ESOPs).

We should also consider that there are some interesting initiatives developed from the "open source" online community; these include the free exchange of information, code, and software offered as open source, including the idea that open source could lead to actual production using 3D printers. The use of "mass" involvement in problem-solving/research activities, free mass online open classes (MOOCs), and "kick-start" financing of projects that avoid banks and financiers in favour of lots of small donations are other Internet community possibilities. Exploring these issues has lead to consideration of the emergence of an "ethical economy" rooted in shared values not value added (Arvidsson & Peitersen, 2013), and a re-opening of the idea of re-occupying "the commons" for the benefit of community co-operation (Zizeck, 2012). It's not clear what will result in terms of work for the mass population from these and other initiatives or if they will successfully resist "monetarization," commercialization, and corporate ownership. These ideas do however present a challenge to corporations and can perhaps exist in "parallel cultures/systems" (Havel et al., 1978) to capitalist structures. We will use the example of another more concrete "parallel" organization, Mondragon, to explore how worker-owned co-operatives can operate and how workers are empowered and can learn within this co-operative context.

Empowerment at Work: The Example of Mondragon

There have always been successful worker and producer co-operative in the USA and Canada. However, the localized and restricted success of worker co-operatives in both countries has dampened enthusiasm for co-operative solutions to unemployment and production problems.[2] Many worker co-operatives exist as a result of a very specific set of circumstances, such as a worker buy-out, or within limited market and capital constraints. For example, the Great Western Brewery in Saskatoon was bought by the workers when Molson pulled out.

The experience in other countries is different, however. For example, in Italy, there are some big worker-managed enterprises; in France, as well, an extensive network of co-operatives is flourishing. There are examples in Portugal and Malta (English & Mayo, 2012, pp. 90-93) and even in Britain the number of worker and community-owned co-operatives is growing, with at least 1,500 currently operating. However, perhaps the best known and most interesting European example of an alternative cooperative "mini-economy" is the Mondragon group of co-operatives in the Basque region of Spain. Much has been written about them, and they do provide an instructive model. They are not perfect—some would argue that they are not even proper worker co-operatives, because of the form of representative democracy (as opposed to direct democracy) used to manage the companies. Nevertheless, the Mondragon co-operatives are a working model of a mini-economy founded on workers' ownership, a form of ownership that excludes external finance (non-working shareholders). They provide, therefore, an example of how workers' control of production might work in practice within a market economy, as well as an example of how larger worker-owned companies can be managed, and is, we believe, worth examining in some detail as an example of a different kind of "employee empowerment."[3]

---

[2] Note, however, that a residue of support exists in a number of locations—for example, most of the support in Canada is in the Atlantic Provinces, Quebec, and Saskatchewan. Actual membership of all types of co-operatives, including credit unions, is high, with an estimated 70% in Quebec and 55% in Saskatchewan and with 4 out of 10 Canadians "belonging" to a co-operative, International Co-operative Alliance, 2010; Canadian Co-operatives Secretariat, 2010. (Most of these are consumer co-ops, not worker-owned.)

[3] They have been described by Greenwood and Santos, in the introduction to their

The Origins: Creating Jobs

The Mondragon co-operative began with the objective of providing work in a depressed area of Spain. During the period 1965-75, they created 1,000 jobs a year and their structures developed as they grew. The enterprises were organized around a structure in which workers possess a capital stake that is paid on entering, and withdrawn on leaving. This rule means that only existing workers can be owners, and yet the numbers employed can expand. Newcomers "buy-in" to specific enterprises with a small capital stake (which may be borrowed from the co-operative bank).

In the Mondragon network, the bank (which was set up three years after the first co-operative and is controlled by the co-operatives), together with the financial and coordinating functions it has spawned, has come to play a pivotal role. These institutions provide financing and coordination between co-operatives, and give support services to would-be co-operative enterprises and to those in financial difficulties.[4] Although crucial, the bank and financial institutions are recognized as secondary to the needs of production, and are therefore established as a secondary co-operative, with both bank and financial employees, and representatives from the producer co-operatives on their governing boards. (Note that the bank was successful in mobilizing workers' savings in much the same way as the early credit unions in Canada.) The co-operatives have created and run their own schools, technical college and university, housing sector, social-security system, and shops.

The success of the linked enterprises provides support for a number of key observations:

- First, workers can run industry without capitalists.
- Second, current production techniques provide an ample surplus for societal needs (in addition to the social provisions mentioned above, 10% of profits go into a social fund).
- Third, resources remain for job creation and retention, and for research and development (Mathews, 2009).

1992 study, as a form of "worker capitalism." This conceptualization is, in our view, a mistaken one because it ignores that the separation of capital and labour, which is so fundamental to capitalism, is absent in Mondragon.

[4] Many have argued that commercial banks and other private sector financial institutions should function in this way rather than just concentrating on building their own profits.

- Finally, most importantly for this book, this example demonstrates that it is possible to integrate work and learning into a genuine employee empowerment.

Although small in scale relative to many large multi-national corporations, Mondragon also illustrates a number of other interesting features and tendencies. For example, the state, or more accurately the local state, can in some respects "wither away" (in relation to its provision of housing, schools, and social security, all of which were taken over by the co-operatives), as new forms of social relations are established.

Running the Co-operatives

Not everyone participates directly in the process of decision-making—there is representative rather than direct democracy, and inevitably, management wields great influence. (Similar tendencies have been seen in many studies of co-operatives in the former Yugoslavia and elsewhere.) However, management is hired and fired by workers, and is treated as part of the workforce, with its pay determined in a way similar to that of other worker-members. There are wage differentials, but they are fixed so that manager-members cannot award themselves bonuses larger than a fixed proportion of the lowest wage. (Currently wage differentials, including managers, have to fit within a 1 to 6 scale—the highest pay rate can be no more than six times the lowest—compared to the 300–400 times greater salary of CEOs in North America!) Also, all workers receive proportional capital benefits that are considerable in size, and that are enjoyed at retirement. Managers tend to be recruited from the local community, and are committed to the co-operatives.

The co-operatives offer increased job security. No firm is taken over (or moved to a low-wage economy) without the knowledge of the workers. No worker can be sacked on a whim of management. Any decision to close (or sell) an enterprise must be agreed to by a general assembly of members, and approved by representatives of the other Mondragon co-operatives. Although there have been some redundancies and closures because of market failure, the linked structure of the co-operatives have allowed workers to find new work in a different co-operative enterprise within the Mondragon group.

Observers have noted a distinction between the democratized forms of governance in Mondragon and more traditional in-work processes within the Mondragon companies. It has been argued that more problem-solving and democratic production processes are needed at a local level in Mondragon to overcome the tendency towards hierarchical problem solving (Greenwood & Santos, 1992).

The Co-operatives during Recession and Growth

If all the Mondragon co-operatives failed together it would be disastrous. At one time, their concentration on domestic consumer products ("white goods") did make them vulnerable. However, more recently, the bank and its offshoot operations act as "minder" of the new and troubled co-operatives. This eliminates unnecessary competition between co-operatives in the group and has stimulated diversification of Mondragon production beyond domestic electrical products. It cannot, of course, isolate the co-operatives from the national or world economy. Studies suggest that the entry of Spain into the European Union and the globalization of transnational competitors are presenting problems, because Mondragon co-operatives have to operate in more competitive markets against exploiters of cheap labour.

The following illustrates this vulnerability to the external economy:

- Mondragon jobs grew even at the outset of the mid-1970s recession, but this growth was checked in the early 1980s, with jobs remaining static (although this record should be compared with a 20% loss in other jobs in the Basque region 1975–83).
- From 1985 to 1989, a 17% growth in co-operative jobs was reported, but the early 1990s saw zero growth as the co-ops consolidated.
- There was rapid expansion of jobs from 1992 (25,322) to 2008 (92,773) but many of these were temporary, non-member jobs.

Paul Phillips (1991) also has reported on a number of changes that the Mondragon co-operatives made in order to adjust to changing market conditions:

- Joint ventures with traditional firms.

- Internal restructuring to match capitalist corporate competitors (stronger sectoral groupings).
- A growth in the size of co-operatives through mergers.

Seeking external finance and the growth of temporary employees could be added to Phillips's list (see Moye, 1993). All of these developments threatened co-operative independence and, as Phillips emphasized, resulted in more remote decision making. At one level, these problems illustrate that co-operatives are perhaps more compatible with a managed government intervention (controls to safeguard co-operative ownership and regulated trade) than with unfettered markets and free trade. However, the changes did create a challenge to the Mondragon ideals (Phillips, 1991; Whyte, 1999).

With many new jobs outside the Basque Country, and even outside of Spain, the majority of the new employees were not co-operative members; many of the new jobs were in distribution and, as noted above, were either part-time or temporary positions. The growth in temporary jobs was a worrying trend with less than a third of all employees being co-op members at its peak, which undermined the co-operative ideal. While these developments were clearly an attempt by the co-operatives to match the cost-cutting tactics of traditional competitors, it struck at the heart of the worker-ownership and employment-creating principles that underpinned Mondragon. In May 2003 the General Assembly of all Mondragon co-operatives approved a resolution regarding "membership expansion," which urged the non-co-operative "spin-off" companies to develop formulas which would enable non-member employees to participate in the ownership and management of their companies. It took a number of years for these programs to be developed but "co-operativization" initiatives were carried out in recent years and this has been successful in achieving the target of more than 75% co-operative membership. By 2011 Mondragon co-operatives were reporting an average of 83,569 people employed per year in more than 250 different companies with 84% of the industrial workforce being co-operative members although this drops to 82% if all distribution employees are included (Mondragon: Humanity at Work, 2012).

The Lessons from Mondragon

How big can such a network grow? Has Mondragon reached its limit? Can it be emulated today? These are open questions. But what this relatively small-scale co-operative economy (surely no longer an experiment) does show is that, for production needs, planning can be undertaken through worker-controlled organizations; in this case, working with the secondary co-operative banking functions. What Mondragon also shows us is that production planning does not have to be bureaucratic or "top-down"; worker-ownership, planning and market choice can operate constructively and harmoniously, under most conditions.

The continued success of Mondragon reputes the idea that workers' control is unable to serve societal needs. Even if, for example, environmental concerns or the interests of minorities were not directly addressed in the first instance, it can be argued that, since the workers live and work in the area and are part of the community, ignoring those needs will eventually directly reflect on them. It is not a remote government or an absentee employer/shareholder who is making the decisions about the nature of work in the locality, or how to dump waste products, but the workers themselves—although operating in hostile market conditions. The data in 2011 showed that Mondragon social funds, environmental initiatives, research and development, education, and training were all growing in real terms.

The co-operatives operated using a team approach before the "team concept" was in general use. However, the changes in work can be overstated, and the actual production processes can be monotonous, with extensive division of labour, perhaps reflecting the discipline of the market. The co-operatives know they must increase the democratization of production processes, and combat the dangers of alienation and apathy some production workers can experience. Studies of other worker co-operatives have concluded that "running a co-operative firm puts worker-owners in a position to make decisions that wouldn't be entertained by ordinary workers—or even board members of an ordinary firm." They know they have to deal with practical issues related to production, questions of equity and sustainability in relation to resources, and to the community (Byrne & Healy, 2006, p. 251).

Mondragon differs from the schemes of wider share ownership, or profit-related pay that are being promoted by some companies. It operates within the limits of the marketplace, but aims to have only those who are currently producing as owning and controlling the companies. There are no absentee shareholders. What is more, the Mondragon co-operatives have a good record of job creation and retention (their original purpose) compared to traditional companies, and has spread from manufacturing and some agriculture production to banking, services, knowledge institutions, housing, and retail. It can be argued they have achieved this growth because their company structure and worker involvement gave them a competitive advantage.

Using the Example

Mondragon is small in scale compared to some large corporations, but it does provide an interesting comparison to privately owned companies seeking new forms of employee participation. It represents a more complete "empowerment," a real extension of democracy (industrial democracy), workers' ownership and control, and the possibility of economic "self-management." These real gains are in contrast to the false "sense" of self-management and ownership claimed as a benefit of new participatory management techniques. At the time of writing it is being tested during the 2012 crisis in Spain but reports suggest Mondragon co-operatives are doing better than average Spanish companies and unemployment in the Basque region is running at less than half the national average. It still serves as an example of an alternative work organization (Wolff, 2012).

The Mondragon co-operatives are not perfect. The form of worker-ownership may be more impressive than the decision-making structures at the level of production. However, Mondragon has made use of a proactive education and training program to ensure that workers participated in formulating, as well as understanding, current policies and remained active participants in the implementation and development of policy. Such attempts might appear to be no different from other companies' "workplace learning" programs, but they are because they exist within a different framework: in the end workers vote for what they want and they hold CEOs accountable.

Mondragon wants all members to have the tools to participate in key investment decisions. Dialogue and debate are valued within Mondragon co-operatives, and this rests on a bed of generally agreed values—solidarity, participation, communication and social justice. These values are not usually associated with privately owned companies, whether or not they are "learning organizations."

Mondragon co-operatives struggle to remain true to their worker-ownership and participation principles during difficult economic conditions but continue to provide a valuable example for others. On October 27, 2009, the United Steelworkers (USW) announced a framework agreement for collaboration in establishing Mondragon-styled co-operatives in the manufacturing sector within the United States and Canada:

> The USW and MONDRAGON will work to establish manufacturing co-operatives that adapt collective bargaining principles to the MONDRAGON worker ownership model of "one worker, one vote." "We see today's agreement as a historic first step towards making union co-ops a viable business model that can create good jobs, empower workers, and support communities in the United States and Canada," said USW International President Leo W. Gerard. "Too often we have seen Wall Street hollow out companies by draining their cash and assets and hollowing out communities by shedding jobs and shuttering plants. We need a new business model that invests in workers and invests in communities." (Dollars and Sense: Real World Economics, October 27, 2009.)

Developments in other countries have also been significant—the growth in co-operatives in Argentina and Brazil being leading examples in South America with 233,000 employees in co-operatives in Argentina, while in Brazil agricultural co-ops produce 40% of agricultural output (International Co-operative Alliance, 2010). One of the threats to the take-over of factories in Argentina and converting them to co-operatives is the threat of the return of the previous owners. This has been met to date by building strong community contacts: contributing to the community culturally and economically (Byrne & Healy, 2006).

Supporters have modestly claimed that Mondragon:

> fits in well with the latest and most advanced management models, which tend to place more value on workers themselves as the principal asset and source of competitive advantage of modern companies (Mondragon: Humanity at Work, 2010).

It can be argued Mondragon goes much further than this insofar as the workers own and control the enterprises; the work, the wealth, and the knowledge belong to them.

References

Agashae, Z. & Bratton, J. (2001). Leader-follower dynamics: Developing a learning organization. *Journal of Workplace Learning 13*(3), 89–102.

Andersson, P. & Harris, J (Eds.) (2006). *Re-theorising the recognition of prior learning.* Leicester, UK: NIACE.

Argyris, C. (1998). Empowerment: The emperor's new clothes. *Harvard Business Review*, May-June, 98–105.

Arvidsson, A. & Peitersen, N. (2013). *The ethical economy.* New York: Columbia University Press.

Bakan, J. (2004). *The corporation: The pathological pursuit of profit and power.* Toronto: Penguin Canada.

Barlow, M. & Robertson, H-J. (1994). *Class warfare: The assault on Canada's schools.* Toronto: Key Porter.

Beattie, A. (1997). *Working people and lifelong learning: A study of the impact of an employee development scheme.* Leicester, UK: NIACE.

Beckstead, D. & Gellatly, G. (2003). *The Canadian economy in transition: The growth and development of new economy industries.* Ottawa: Minister of Industry. 11-622-MIE no.002.

Belenky, M., Clinchy, B., Goldberger, N., & Tarule, J. (1986). *Women's ways of knowing: The development of self, mind, and voice.* New York: Basic Books.

Bernhardt, A., Dresser, L., & Rogers, J. (2004). Taking the high road in Milwaukee: The Wisconsin Regional Training Partnership. *WorkingUSA, 5*(3), 109–30.

Berry-Loud, D., Rowe, V. & Parsons, D. (2001) *Recent developments in employee development schemes.* London: DfES Report RR310.

Bloom, A. (1987). *The closing of the American mind.* New York: Simon & Schuster.

Boreham, N., Samurcay, R. & Fisher, M (Eds.) (2002). *Work process knowledge.* London: Routledge.

Bouchard, P. (1998). Training and work: Myths about human capital. In S. Scott, B. Spencer, & A. Thomas (Eds.). *Learning for life: Canadian readings in adult education* (pp. 128–39). Toronto: Thompson Educational Publishing.

Bouchard, P. (2006). Human capital and the knowledge economy. In T. Fenwick, T. Nesbit & B. Spencer (Eds.). *Contexts of adult education: Canadian perspectives* (pp. 164–172). Toronto: Thompson Educational Publishing.

Boud, D. & Garrick, J. (Eds.) (1999). *Understanding learning at work.* London: Routledge.

Bowles, S. & Gintis, H. (1976). *Schooling in capitalist America.* London: Routledge & Kegan Paul.

Bratton, J. (1992). *Japanization at work*. London: Macmillan.

Bratton, J. (1999). *Gaps in the workplace learning paradigm: Labour flexibility and job design, Researching work and learning: A first international conference*, 486–92. Leeds: School of Continuing Education, Leeds University.

Bratton, J. & Gold, J. (2012) *Human resource management: Theory and practice* (5th ed.). Basingstoke: Palgrave Macmillan.

Bratton, J., Helms-Mills, J., Pyrch, T., & Sawchuk, P. (2004). *Workplace learning: A critical introduction*. Aurora, ON: Garamond Press.

Briton, D., Gereluk, W., & Spencer, B. (1998). Prior learning assessment and recognition: Issues for adult educators (pp. 24–28). In *CASAE Conference Proceedings*.

Brookfield, S. (1987). *Developing critical thinkers*. San Francisco: Jossey-Bass.

Brookfield, S. (2005) *The power of critical theory: Liberating adult learning and teaching*. San Francisco: Jossey-Bass.

Brown, T. (1999). *Restructuring the workplace: Case studies of informal economic learning*. Sydney: Centre for Popular Education, University of Technology.

Burbules, N. & Berk, R. (1999). Critical thinking and critical pedagogy: Relations, differences, and limits. In T. Popkewitz, & L. Fendler (Eds.) *Critical theories in education: Changing terrains of knowledge and politics* (pp. 45–65). New York: Routledge.

Byrd, B. & Nissen, B. (2003). *Report on the state of labor education in the United States*. Berkeley, CA: Center for Labor Research and Education.

Byrne, K. & Healy, S. (2006). Co-operative subjects: Towards a post-fantasmatic enjoyment of the economy. *Rethinking Marxism* 18(2), 241–58.

Canadian Centre for Policy Alternatives. (2012). *The clash for cash: CEOs v the average Joe*. Retrieved from: www.policyalternatives.ca/ceo

Canadian Co-operatives Secretariat. (2010). Retrieved from: www.mondragon-corporation.com/language/en-US/ENG.aspx

Cervero, R. & Wilson, A. (2006). *Working the planning table: Negotiating democratically for adult, continuing and workplace education*. San Francisco: Jossey-Bass.

CIA World Fact-book. (2012). Retrieved from: www.cia.gov/library/publications/the-world-factbook/

Clegg, H. (1978). *Trade unions under collective bargaining*. Oxford: Basil Blackwell.

Clegg, S. (2005). Evidence-based practice in educational research: A critical realist critique of systematic review. *British Journal of Sociology of Education*, 26(3), 415–42.

Coffield, F. (1999). Breaking the consensus: lifelong learning as social control. *British Journal of Educational Research* 25(4), 479–99.

Cohen, M. (Ed.) (2003). *Training the excluded for work: Access and equity for women, immigrants, First Nations, youth, and people with low incomes.* Vancouver: UBC Press.

Collini, S. (2012). *What are universities for?* Penguin: London.

Collins, M. (1991). *Adult education as vocation: A critical role for the adult educator.* New York: Routledge.

Contenta, S. (1993). *Rituals of failure.* Toronto: Between the Lines.

Cooper, L. & Walters, S. (Eds.) (2009). *Learning/Work: Turning work and learning inside out.* Cape Town: Human Sciences Research Council Press.

Critoph, U. (2003). Who wins, who loses: The real story of the transfer of training to the provinces and its impact on women. In Cohen, M. (Ed), *Training the excluded for work: Access and equity for women, immigrants, First Nations, youth, and people with low incomes.* Vancouver: UBC Press.

Cruikshank, J. (2006). Lifelong learners and the new economy: Voices of workers (pp. 33–38). *Proceedings of the 25th annual CASAE conference.*

Curtis, B. (1988). *Building the educational state: Canada West, 1836–1871.* London: The Falmer Press.

Davies, B. (2003). Death to critique and dissent? The politics and practices of new managerialism and of "evidence-based practice." *Gender and Education,* 15(10), 91–103.

Davies, B. (2005). Winning hearts and minds of academics in the service of neo-liberalism. *Dialogue,* 24, 26–37.

Davies, B., & Petersen, E. B. (2005). Neo-liberal discourse in the academy: The forestalling of (collective) resistance. *LATISS – Learning and Teaching in the Social Sciences, 2*(2), 77–98.

Delbridge, R. & Keenoy, T. (2010). Beyond managerialism? *The International Journal of Human Resource Management,* 21(6), 799–817.

Deneault, A. (2011). *Offshore: Tax havens, criminal enterprise, and the growing global threat to our democracy* (English translation). New York: New Press.

Dollars and Sense: Real World Economics, (2009). Retrieved from: www.dollarsandsense.org/blog/2009/10/steelworkers-form-collaboration-with.html.

Drucker, P. (1964). *Managing for results.* London: Heinemann.

Du Gay, P. (1996a). *Consumption and identity at work.* London: Sage.

Du Gay, P. (1996b). Organizing identity: Entrepreneurial governance and public management. In S. Hall & P. Du Gay. (Eds.). *Questions of cultural identity* (pp. 151–169). London: Sage.

Ellerman, D. (1990). *The democratic worker-owned firm.* Winchester: Unwin Hyman.

English, L. & Mayo, P. (2012). *Learning with adults: A critical pedagogical introduction.* Rotterdam: Sense Publishers.

Erwin, L. & MacLennan, D. (1994). *Sociology of education in Canada.* Toronto: Copp Clark Longman.

European Commission (2002). *Social inclusion through APEL: A Learners Perspective. Comparative Report.* Glasgow: Glasgow Caledonian University.

Fenwick, T. (2006a). Work, learning and adult education in Canada. In T. Fenwick, T. Nesbit & B. Spencer (Eds.) *Contexts of adult education: Canadian perspectives* (pp. 187–97). Toronto: Thompson Educational Publishing.

Fenwick, T. (2006b). Control, contradiction and ambivalence: Skill initiatives in Canada. *CASAE conference proceedings*, Toronto OISE. Retrieved from: www.ualberta.ca/~tfenwick/publications/PDF/CASAE.pdf

Field, L. (2004). Rethinking "organisational learning." In G. Foley (Ed.), *Dimensions of adult learning: Adult education and training in a global era* (pp. 201–18). Crows Nest, New South Wales: Allen and Unwin.

Finkel, A. & Conrad, M. (1993). *History of the Canadian peoples: 1867 to the present*, vol 2. Mississauga, ON: Copp Clark Pitman.

Forrester, K. (1999). *Work-related learning and the struggle for subjectivity, in researching work and learning: A first international conference* (pp. 188–97). Leeds: School of Continuing Education, Leeds University.

Forrester, K. (2002). Unions and workplace learning: The British experience. In Spencer, B. (Ed.) *Unions and learning in a global economy: International and comparative perspectives* (pp. 138–48). Toronto: Thompson Educational Publishing.

Forrester, K (2004). Workplace learning. In G. Foley. *Dimensions of adult learning: Adult education and training in a global era* (pp. 219–25). NSW, Australia: Allen & Unwin.

Forrester, K. & Li, H. C. (2009). Learning, practice and democracy: Exploring union learning. In L. Cooper & S. Walters (Eds.). *Learning/Work: Turning work and learning inside out.* Cape Town: Human Sciences Research Council Press

Freedland, J. (2006). Market rule will cook us all. *Guardian Weekly*, Nov 3–9, p. 5.

Freedman, J. (1995). *The charter school idea: Breaking educational gridlock.* Red Deer, AB: Society for Advancing Educational Research.

Freeman, R., Boxall, P. & Haynes, P. (Eds.) (2007). *What workers say: Employee voice in the Anglo-American workplace.* New York: Cornell University.

Freire, P. (1970). *Pedagogy of the oppressed.* New York: Continuum.

Friesen, J. & Friesen. V. (2001). *In Defense of public school in North America.* Calgary, AB: Temeron/Detselig.

Goldenberg, M. (2006). *Employer investment in workplace learning in Canada.* Canadian Council on Learning. Retrieved from: www.ccl-cca.ca/NR/rdonlyres/4F86830F-D201-4CAF-BA12-333B51CEB988/0/EmployerInvestmentWorkplaceLearningCCLCPRN.pdf

Greenwood, D., & Santos, J. (1992). *Industrial democracy as process.* Stockholm: Swedish Centre for Working Life.

Gutek, G. (1997). *Philosophical and ideological perspectives on education* (2nd ed.). Needham Heights, MA: Allyn & Bacon, Inc.

Habermas, J. (1972). *Knowledge and human interests.* London: Heinemann. (Original work published 1968).

Hall, G. (2004). *Why you can't do cultural studies and be a Derridean: Cultural studies after Birmingham, the new social movements and the new left.* Retrieved from: http://culturemachine.tees.ac.uk/frm_f1.htm

Hanson, K. (1997). A university perspective on PLA. *Learning Quarterly, 1*(3), 10–13.

Hart, M. (1995). *Working and educating for life: Feminist and international perspectives on adult education.* London: Routledge.

Havel, V. et al (1978, 1985 Ed. J Kean). *The power of the powerless: Citizens against the state in central-eastern Europe.* Armonk, NY: M. E. Sharpe.

Hennessy, T. & Sawchuk, P. (2003). Technological change in the Canadian public sector: Worker learning responses and openings for labour-centric technological development. In *The third international conference of researching work and learning* (pp. 111–19). Tampere, Finland: University of Tampere.

Henry, J. (2012). *The price of offshore revisited.* Retrieved from: www.taxjustice.net/cms/upload/pdf/Price_of_Offshore_Revisited_120722.pdf

Honderich, T. (2002). *After the terror.* Edinburgh: University Press.

Honold, L. (1991). *The power of learning at Johnsonville foods.* Training, April, 55–58.

Howell, S., Preston, J., Schied, F., & Carter, V. (1996). Creating a learning organization, creating a controlling organization: A case study of total quality management in an industrial setting. In *37th Annual adult education research conference* (pp. 169–74). Tampa: University of South Florida.

Hughes, P. & Grant, M. (2007). *Learning and development outlook: Are we learning enough?* Toronto: Conference Board of Canada.

Human Resources and Skills Development Canada (2007, Oct). *Determinants of formal and informal Canadian adult learning: Insights from the adult education and training Surveys.* Retrieved from: www.rhdcc-hrsdc.gc.ca/eng/publications_resources/research/categories/llsd/2007/sp_792_10_07/page04.shtml

International Co-operative Alliance. (2010). Retrieved from: www.ica.coop/coop/statistics.html

International Labour Organization. (2007). Strengthening the trade unions: The key role of labour education. *Labour Education,* 1–2, 146–47.

Issues for adult educators. *CASAE Conference Proceedings* (pp. 24–28). Ottawa: University of Ottawa.

Jackson. A. (2005). Productivity and building human capital for the "bottom third" *International productivity monitor,* (11, Fall). Retrieved from: www.csls.ca/ipm/11/IPM-11-jackson-e.pdf

Jackson, N. & Jordan, S. (2000). Learning for work: Contested terrain? *Studies in the Education of Adults* 32(2), 195–211.

Jackson, P. (1968). *Life in classrooms.* Eastbourne, UK: Holt Rinehart & Winston.

Jones, G. A. (2004). Ontario higher education reform, 1995–2003: From modest modifications to policy reform. *The Canadian Journal of Higher Education, XXXIV*(3), 39–54.

Judge, M. (Director). (1999). *Office Space* [Motion picture]. United States: Twentieth Century Fox Film Corporation.

Kelly, J. (1998). *Under the gaze: Learning to be black in white society.* Halifax: Fernwood.

Kelly, J. (2004). *Borrowed identities.* New York: Peter Lange.

Kelly, J. & Cui, D. (2012). Racialization and work. In Finkel, A, (Ed.). *Working people in Alberta: A history* (pp. 267–86). Edmonton: Athabasca University Press.

Kelly, J., & Yochim, L. (2011). Learning and the "circuit of culture": A cultural exploration and reflection on the university as a work site. *Canadian Journal for the Study of Adult Education, 24*(1), 1–14.

Kennedy, H. (1995). *Return to learn: UNISON's fresh approach to trade union education.* London: UNISON.

Kersley, B., Alpin, C., Forth, J., Bryson, A., Bewley, H., Dix, G. & Oxenbridge, S. (2006). *Inside the Workplace: Findings from the 2004 Workplace Employment Relations.* Survey. London: Routledge.

Kincheloe, J. (1999). *How do we tell the workers? The socioeconomic foundations of work and vocational education.* Boulder, CO: Westview Press.

Klein, J. A. (1989). The human costs of manufacturing reform. *Harvard Business Review, 67*(2), 60–66.

Klein, N. (2000). *No logo: Taking aim at the brand bullies.* Toronto: Random House.

Klein, N. (2007). *The shock doctrine: The rise of disaster capitalism.* Toronto: Alfred A. Knopf.

Lather, P. (1991). *Getting smart: Feminist research and pedagogy within the postmodern.* New York: Routledge.

LeCompte, M. (1978). Learning to work: The hidden curriculum of the classroom. *Anthropology and Education Quarterly, 9*(1), 22–37.

Lee, C. (1999). *Learning from employee development schemes.* London: Employment Brief no 41. Institute for Employment Studies.

Li. C, Gervais, G., & Duval, A. (2006). *The dynamics of overqualification: Canada's unemployed university graduates.* Ottawa: Statistics Canada. Retrieved from: www.statcan.gc.ca/pub/11-621-m/11-621-m2006039-eng.pdf

Livingstone, D. (1999a). *The education-jobs gap: Underemployment or economic democracy.* Toronto: Garamond Press.

Livingstone, D. (1999b). Exploring the icebergs of adult learning: Findings of the first Canadian survey of informal learning practices. *CJSAE 13*(2), 49–72.

Livingstone, D. & Sawchuk, P. (2004). *Hidden knowledge: Organized labour in the information age.* Aurora, ON: Garamond Press.

Loach, K. (Director). (2000). *Bread and Roses* [Motion picture]. United Kingdom: Parallax Pictures.

Louge, J. & McCarthy, C. (2007). Shooting the elephant: Antagonistic identities, and neo-Marxist nostalgia, and the remorselessly vanishing pasts. In C. McCarthy, A. Durham, L. Engle, A. Filmer, M. Giardina, & M. Malagreca (Eds.). *Globalizing cultural studies: Ethnographic interventions in theory, method and policy* (pp. 3–22). New York: Peter Lang.

Lowe, G. (2000). *Quality of work: A people-centred agenda.* Don Mills, ON: Oxford University Press.

Lynch, K. (2010, 30 Jan). Canada's productivity trap. *Globe & Mail* (Feature article).

Macklem, K. (2002, December 30). Crooks in the boardroom. *Maclean's.*

Maclachlan, K. (1999, Nov). *Learning Works: A view from within,* Glasgow: Learning Works, University of Glasgow.

Marsick, V. & Watkins, K. (1999). Envisioning new organizations for learning. In D. Boud & J Garrick, (Eds.). *Understanding learning at work* (pp. 199–215). London: Routledge.

Martin, M. (2012, Feb 17). Cooperative success confounds liberals, analysts alike, *The Exponent-On-line.* Retrieved from: www.purdueexponent.org/campus/article_cea97626-7952-521c-a743-6d798191d245.html

Mathews, R. (2009). *Jobs of our own: Building a stakeholder society, alternatives to the market and the state.* Irving, TX: Distributist Review Press.

Meen, S. (1999). Putting PLAR at the heart: A case study of a university degree program designed for DaimlerChrysler employees. PLAR 99 Conference. Vancouver.

Meighan, R. (1981). *A sociology of education.* London: Holt Rinehart & Winston.

Mezirow, J. (1981). A critical theory of adult learning and education. *Adult Education 32*(1), 3–21.

Miller, D. (2012). *Last nightshift in Savar: The story of the Spectrum Sweater factory collapse.* Alnwick (Northumberland, England): McNidder & Grace.

Mirchandani, K., Ng, R., Colomo-Moya, N., Maitra, S., Rawlings, T., Shan, H., Siddiqui, K., & Slade, B. (2008). Transitions into precarious work: Immigrants' learning and resistance. In D. Livingstone, K. Mirchandani, & P. Sawchuk (Eds.). *The Future of Lifelong Learning and Work: Critical Perspectives* (pp. 171–184). Rotterdam: Sense Publishers.

Mirchandani, K., Ng, R., Colomo-Moya, N., Maitra, S., Rawlings, T., Shan, H., Siddiqui, K., & Slade, B. (2010). Transitions into precarious work: Immigrants' learning and resistance. In P. Sawchuk & A. Taylor (Eds.) *Challenging transitions in learning and work: Reflections on policy and practice* (pp. 231–42). Rotterdam: Sense Publishers.

Mirchandani, K & Slade, B. (2002). Constructing resistance: A geo-cultural analysis on promotional material on home-based work. Proceedings of the 21st annual CASAE conference, (pp. 188–193).

Misham, E. J. (1967, 1969ed). *The costs of economic growth.* Harmondsworth: Pelican Books.

Mitchell, K. (2003). Educating the national citizen in neo-liberal times: from the multicultural self to the strategic cosmopolitan. *Transactions of the Institute of British Geographers, 28*(4), 387–403.

Mojab, S., & Gorman, R. (2003). Women and consciousness in the "learning organization": Emancipation or exploitation? *Adult Education Quarterly 53*(4), 228–41.

Mondragon: Humanity at Work. (2010). Retrieved from: www.mondragon-corporation.com/language/en-US/ENG.aspx.

Moore, M. (Director). (2007). *Sicko* [Motion picture]. United States: Dog Eat Dog Films.

Moye, A. (1993). Mondragon: Adapting co-operative structures to meet the demands of a changing environment, *Economic and Industrial Democracy, 14*(2), 251–76.

Murphy, S. (1994). "No-one has ever grown taller as a result of being measured" – Six educational measurement lessons for Canadians. In L. Erwin & D. MacLennan (Eds.). *Sociology of education in Canada: Critical perspectives on theory, research and practice* (pp. 228–52). Toronto: Copp Clark Longman.

Nikiforuk, A. (1993). *School's out: The catastrophe in public education and what we can do about it.* Toronto: MacFarlane, Walter & Ross.

Nolan, P. (2011). Money, markets, meltdown: The 21st century crisis of labour. *Industrial Relations Journal, 42*(1), 2–17.

Olssen, M., & Peters, M. A. (2005). Neoliberalism, higher education and the knowledge economy: From free market to knowledge capitalism, *Journal of Education Policy, 20*(3), 313–345.

Parsons, D., Cocks, N., & Rowe, V. (1998). *The role of employee development schemes in increasing learning at work.* London: Department for Education and Employment.

Patel, R. (2009). *The value of nothing.* Toronto: Harper-Collins.

Perkins, J. (2006). *Confessions of an economic hit man.* New York: Plume Books.

Peruniak, G. (1997). Dimensions of competence-based learning. In S. Scott, B. Spencer, & A. Thomas (Eds.). *Learning for life: Canadian readings in adult education* (pp. 313–29). Toronto: Thompson Educational Publishing.

Peters, H. (2001). *The "trojan horse": Can recognition of prior learning be used as a means of bringing about change from within in traditional institutions of higher education?* SCUTREA University of East London.

Peters, H., Pokorny, H. & Sheibani, A. (1999). *Fitting in: What place is accorded to the experiential learning the mature students bring with them to higher education.* SCUTREA University of Warwick.

Phillips, P. (1991, March). Is industrial democracy feasible? Lessons from Mondragon, *Canadian Dimension*, 38–41.

Pizzigati, S. (2004). *Greed and good: Understanding and overcoming the inequality that limits our lives.* New York: Apex Press.

Prentice, A. (1977). *The school promoters: Education and social class in mid-nineteenth century Upper Canada.* Toronto: McClelland & Stewart.

Probert, B. (1999). Gendered workers and gendered work: Implications for women's learning (p. 98). In Boud, D, & Garrick, J. *Understanding learning at work.* London: Routledge.

Robertson, D., Rienhart, J. & Huxley, C. (1989). Team concept and kaizen: Japanese production in a unionised Canadian auto plant. *Studies in Political Economy* 39, 77–107.

Robertson, H-J. (2007). *Great expectations: Essays on schools and society.* Ottawa: Canadian Centre for Policy Alternatives.

Russell, E. & Dufour, M. (2007). *Rising profit shares, falling wages shares, Canadian Centre for Policy Alternatives.* Retrieved from: www.policyalternatives.ca/sites/default/files/uploads/publications/National_Office_Pubs/2007/Rising_Profit_Shares_Falling_Wage_Shares.pdf

Salamon, L. (2003). *The resilient sector: The state of nonprofit America.* Washington, DC: Brookings Institution.

Sawchuk, P. (2001). Trade unions-based workplace learning: A case study in workplace reorganization and worker knowledge production. *Journal of Workplace Learning, 13*(7/8), 344–51.

Sawchuk, P. (2003). *Adult learning and technology in working-class life.* Cambridge: Cambridge University Press.

Sawchuk, P. (2008) Lifelong learning and work as 'value' production: Combining work and learning analysis from a cultural historical perspective. In D. Livingstone, K Mirchandani, & P Sawchuk, (Eds) *The future of lifelong learning and work: Critical perspectives* (pp. 73–84). Rotterdam: Sense Publishers.

Sawchuk, P. (2010). Occupational transitions within workplaces undergoing change: A case study from the public sector. In P. Sawchuk & A. Taylor (Eds.). *Challenging transitions in learning and work: Reflections on policy and practice* (pp. 189–208). Sense Publishers.

Sawchuk, P. (2011). Researching workplace learning: An overview and critique. In M. Malloch, L. Cairns, K. Evans and B. O'Connor (Eds.). *The Sage handbook of workplace learning* (pp. 141–53). London: Sage.

Sawchuk, P. & Taylor, A. (Eds.). (2010). *Challenging transitions in learning and work: Reflections on policy and practice.* Rotterdam: Sense Publishers.

Schein, E. (1985). *Organizational culture and leadership.* San Francisco: Jossey-Bass.

Schied, F., Carter, V., Preston, J., and Howell, S. (1997a). Knowledge as "quality non-conformance": A critical case study of ISO 9000 and adult education in the workplace. *38th annual adult education research conference* (pp. 214–19). Stillwater, Oklahoma: Oklahoma State University.

Schied, F., Carter, V., Preston, J., and Howell, S. (1997b). The HRD factory: An historical inquiry into the production of control in the workplace. Crossing boarders breaking boundaries. *Research in the education of adults: An international conference* (pp. 404–08). London: Birkbeck College, University of London.

Schissel, B. & Wotherspoon, T. (2003). *The legacy of school for Aboriginal people: Education, oppression and emancipation.* Toronto: Oxford UP.

Schultz, T. W. (1961). Investment in human capital. In M. Blaug, (Ed.). *Economics of education.* London: Penguin.

Schwind, H., Das, H., & Wagar, T. (2007). *Canadian human resource management: A strategic approach,* (8th ed.). Whitby, ON: McGraw-Hill Ryerson.

Scipes, K. (2011). *Understanding the occupy movement.* Retrieved from: www.countercurrents.org/scipes311211.htm

Selman, G. (1998). The imaginative training for citizenship. In S. Scott, B. Spencer, & A. Thomas (Eds.). *Learning for life: Canadian readings in adult education,* (pp. 24–34). Toronto: Thompson Educational Publishing.

Selman, G., Cooke, M. Selman, & Dampier, P. (1998). *The foundations of adult education in Canada.* Toronto: Thompson Educational Publishing.

Senge, P. (1990a). *The fifth discipline: The art and practice of the learning organization.* New York: Doubleday.

Senge, P. (1990b). The leaders new work: Building learning organizations. *Sloan Management Review,* Fall 7–23.

Sennett, R. (1998) *The corrosion of character: the personal consequences of work in the new capitalism.* New York: W. W. Norton & Co.

Sensoy, O. & DiAngelo, R. (2012). *Is everyone really equal? An introduction to key concepts in social justice education.* New York: Teachers College Press.

Shaffer, H. (1961). A critique of the concept of human capital. In M. Blaug, (Ed.). *Economics of education.* London: Penguin.

Shelley, S & Calveley, M, (Eds.). (2007). *Learning with trade unions: A contemporary agenda in employment relations.* Aldershot, UK: Ashgate.

Slade, B. & Schugurensky, D. (2010). "Starting from another side, the bottom": Volunteer work as a transition into the labour market for immigrant professionals. In P. Sawchuk & A. Taylor (Eds.) *Challenging transitions in learning and work: Reflections on policy and practice* (pp. 261–81). Rotterdam: Sense Publishers.

Solomon, N. (1999). Culture and difference in workplace learning. In D. Boud & J. Garrick (Eds.). *Understanding learning at work (*pp. 119–131). London: Routledge.

Solomon, N. (2001). Workplace learning as a cultural technology. In Fenwick, T. *Sociocultural perspectives on learning through work* (pp. 41–52). San Francisco: Jossey-Bass.

Spencer, B. (1989). *Remaking the working class?* Nottingham: Spokesman.

Spencer, B. (2006). *The purposes of adult education: A short introduction.* Toronto: Thompson Educational Publishing.

Spencer, B. (Ed.). (2002). *Unions and learning in a global economy: International and comparative perspectives.* Toronto: Thompson Educational Publishing.

Spencer, B. & Kelly, J. (2005 printed 2007). Is Workplace Learning Higher Education? *Canadian Journal for the Study of Adult Education* 2(19), 33–51.

Spencer, B. & Lange, E. (2013). *The purposes of adult education: A short introduction* (revised edition). Toronto: Thompson Educational Press.

Statistics Canada. (2012). Retrieved from: www.statcan.gc.ca/start-debut-eng.html.

Steele, T. (1997). *The emergence of cultural studies: Adult education, cultural politics and the "English" question.* London: Lawrence and Wishart.

Storey, J. (2001). *Human resource management: A critical text* (2nd ed.), London: Thomson Learning.

Storey, J. (2007). *Human resource management: A critical text* (3rd ed.), London: Thomson Learning.

Storey, J., Wright, P., & Ulrich, D. (Eds.). (2009) *The Routledge Companion to Strategic Human Resource Management.* New York: Routledge.

Stryke, D. (2011). *Iceland's on-going revolution.* Retrieved from: www.positivenewsus.org/editions/fal11/fal1105.html

Swift, J. (1995). *Wheel of fortune: Work and life in the age of falling expectations.* Toronto: Between the Lines.

Taylor, A. & Watt-Malcolm, B. (2008). Building a future for high school students in trades. In Livingstone, D., Mirchandani, K. & Sawchuk, P. *The future of lifelong learning and work: Critical perspectives.* Rotterdam: Sense Publishers.

Taylor, M. (Ed.). (1997). *Workplace education: The changing landscape.* Toronto: Culture Concepts.

Taylor, R., Barr, J. & Steele, T. (2002). *For a radical higher education: After postmodernism.* Buckingham, UK: The Society for Research into Higher Education & Open University Press.

Terkel, S. (1977, first published in 1974). *Working: People talk about what they do and how they feel about what they do.* New York: New Press

Thomas, A. (1998). The tolerable contradictions of prior learning assessment. In S. Scott, B. Spencer, & A. Thomas (Eds.). *Learning for life: Canadian readings in adult education,* (pp. 354–64). Toronto: Thompson Educational Publishing.

Thompson. E. P. (1970). *Warwick University Ltd.* Penguin Education: London.

Tough, A. (1979). *The adult's learning projects: A fresh approach to theory and practice in adult learning.* Toronto: OISE.

Trade Union Congress. (2009). *Unfair to middling.* London: TUC.

University of Leeds, School of Continuing Education (Feb 2001). *Exploring employee learning in "Learning for Life"* (Evaluation report–Learning for Life scheme), Leeds: author.

Waters, M. (1994). *Modern sociological theory.* London: Sage.

Wellins, R., Byham, W. & Wilson, J. (1991). *Empowered teams: Creating self-directed work groups that improve quality, productivity and participation.* San Francisco: Jossey-Bass.

Wells, D. (1993). Are strong unions compatible with the new model of human resource management, *Relations Industrielles/Industrial Relations, 48*(1), 56–84.

Welton, M. (1991). *Toward development work: The workplace as a learning environment.* Geelong, Australia: Deakin University Press.

Welton, M, (2005). *Designing the just learning society: A critical inquiry.* Leicester, UK: NIACE.

Whyte, W. F. (1999). The Mondragon co-operatives in 1976 and 1998. *Industrial and Labour Relations Review, 52*(3), 478–81.

Willis, P. (1977). *Learning to labor: How working class kids get working class jobs.* New York: Columbia University Press

Wilkinson, A. (1998). Empowerment: theory and practice. *Personnel Review 27*(1), 40–56.

Wiltshire, H (1980). *The 1919 Report.* Nottingham: The Department of Adult Education, University of Nottingham.

Wolff, R, (2012, 24 June). Yes, there is an alternative to capitalism: Mondragon shows the way. *The Guardian.*

Wotherspoon, T. (2009). *The sociology of education in Canada: Critical perspectives.* Toronto: Oxford UP.

Wray, D. (2001). What price partnership? Unpublished paper presented at Work Employment and Society Conference, 11–13 Sept, University of Nottingham.

Zimmerman, A. (2004, March 26). Costco's dilemma: Be kind to its workers, or Wall Street? *The Wall Street Journal,* p B1. Retrieved from: http://online.wsj.com/article_email/0,,SB108025917854365904-INjeoNplaV3oJ2pan2IbauIm4,00.html

Zizeck, S. (2012). *The year of dreaming dangerously.* London: Verso.

Index

P

M

N

P

S

T

U

W